AI MARKETING MASTERY

Techniques for Success

By
Cameron Blake

AI Marketing Mastery

Techniques for Success

CONTENTS

INTRODUCTION

Welcome to a transformative journey where artificial intelligence (AI) meets the ever-evolving world of marketing. The confluence of AI and marketing isn't just a buzzword; it's a paradigm shift that's reshaping how businesses engage with their customers, drive engagement, and achieve measurable outcomes. For marketing professionals and enthusiasts alike, understanding and harnessing the power of AI can be the key to unlocking new levels of effectiveness and innovation.

Artificial intelligence offers a wealth of opportunities for marketers, from enhancing customer segmentation to automating campaigns and delivering personalized experiences. But before diving into these advanced techniques, it's vital to grasp the foundational concepts. This book aims to lay that groundwork, while also guiding you through sophisticated applications and strategies to fully leverage AI in your marketing efforts.

The integration of AI in marketing isn't a one-size-fits-all approach. Different industries, businesses, and even marketing channels require tailored strategies. This book is designed to help you navigate these intricacies, providing you with practical insights and actionable techniques regardless of your current level of AI familiarity. Whether you're a seasoned professional looking to stay ahead of the curve or a curious beginner aiming to get your foot in the door, there's something here for everyone.

AI's potential in marketing is immense, yet understanding where to start can be a daunting task. That's why we'll begin with the basics—breaking down complex AI concepts into understandable, relatable terms. From there, we'll explore the historical evolution of marketing with AI, unveiling how it's reshaped traditional marketing practices into data-driven, highly efficient systems.

In today's competitive landscape, data is more valuable than ever. AI allows marketers to delve deeper into data-driven insights, transforming raw information into actionable intelligence. This comprehensive approach ensures you're making informed decisions, improving customer segmentation, and targeting with unparalleled precision. By grasping the importance of effective data utilization, you secure a robust foundation for your AI marketing strategies.

Personalization has become the cornerstone of modern marketing, and AI is taking it to new heights. Brands can no longer afford to deliver generic messages; AI enables hyper-personalized interactions that resonate with customers on an individual level. This personalization fosters a sense of loyalty and increases engagement, driving better outcomes.

As automation becomes more sophisticated, the efficiency and effectiveness of marketing campaigns surge. Automated email marketing, social media strategies, and other campaign types benefit immensely from AI, which can manage and optimize these processes in real-time. This book will detail the nuances of setting up and fine-tuning AI-driven campaigns to ensure they achieve maximum impact.

Customer service also experiences a significant transformation with AI. Chatbots and virtual assistants can handle a multitude of customer inquiries, providing instant responses and freeing up human agents for more complex tasks. The seamless integration of AI in customer service enhances the overall customer experience, driving satisfaction and loyalty.

Predictive analytics is another area where AI excels, making it possible to forecast trends, customer behavior, and campaign outcomes with remarkable accuracy. This predictive power allows marketers to stay ahead of the game, adapting strategies proactively and efficiently. It's about predicting what customers will want before they even know they want it.

Content creation, often a time-consuming part of marketing, is revolutionized by AI. From generating articles to crafting compelling copies, AI tools can produce content that not only saves time but also maintains high quality and relevance. This ensures a consistent brand voice and quicker turnaround times for marketing materials.

SEO strategies have also seen a shift with AI integration. The algorithms that drive search engine rankings are increasingly sophisticated, and AI tools can help decipher these complexities. Marketers can optimize their content and websites more effectively, driving organic traffic and improving visibility.

Advertising hasn't been left behind in the AI revolution. Programmatic advertising, a technique that uses AI to buy and place ads, ensures that marketing budgets are spent efficiently. Ad targeting and optimization further enhance the relevance and impact of ads, reaching the right audience at the right time.

Influencer marketing, too, benefits from AI. Identifying the right influencers, measuring their impact, and optimizing influencer campaigns become more manageable tasks with AI tools. These technologies can analyze vast amounts of data to determine the best influencers who align with your brand and audience.

Customer loyalty programs are evolving to be more dynamic and personalized thanks to AI. These programs can now offer tailored rewards and experiences that genuinely resonate with customers, driving loyalty and repeat business.

As we delve into sentiment analysis, marketers gain a deeper understanding of customer opinions and emotions. AI can analyze customer feedback and social media conversations at scale, providing insights that help refine marketing strategies and improve customer relationships.

Market research, once a tedious and labor-intensive process, is streamlined with AI. These tools can analyze trends, competitor strategies, and market dynamics more rapidly, providing marketers with the intelligence needed to stay competitive.

However, with great power comes great responsibility. The use of AI in marketing raises important ethical questions and concerns about privacy. This book will address these issues, providing guidelines for responsible AI use that ensures consumer trust and regulatory compliance.

To effectively harness AI, marketers need to understand the tools and platforms available. This book will introduce you to a variety of AI tools tailored for different marketing needs, equipping you with the knowledge to choose the right ones for your business.

Small businesses can also reap the benefits of AI. This book will show you how to implement AI solutions on a budget, ensuring that enterprises of all sizes can compete on a level playing field.

Real-world case studies offer valuable lessons and insights. We'll explore various industries, such as retail and financial services, to see how they're successfully integrating AI into their marketing strategies. These case studies serve as tangible examples of theory put into practice.

No marketing strategy is complete without measuring return on investment (ROI). AI provides sophisticated tools for tracking and analyzing the success of marketing efforts, ensuring that resources are used efficiently and effectively.

Of course, the journey to AI integration is not without challenges. We'll address common hurdles and provide solutions to overcome them, ensuring a smoother transition for your marketing strategies.

Looking ahead, future trends in AI marketing promise exciting possibilities. Staying informed about these developments ensures you're always at the cutting edge of marketing innovation.

Integrating AI with traditional marketing strategies can create a more holistic and effective approach. This book will guide you on how to blend these methods seamlessly.

Building a skilled AI marketing team is crucial. The right talent can make or break your AI initiatives, and we'll provide strategies for assembling a team that's equipped to drive AI success.

Finally, we'll help you develop a comprehensive AI-driven marketing strategy. By the end of this book, you'll have the tools, knowledge, and confidence to integrate AI into your marketing efforts and achieve remarkable results.

CHAPTER 1:
UNDERSTANDING AI IN MARKETING

The rise of artificial intelligence (AI) in marketing isn't just a trend; it's an evolution. As a marketing professional, one can't afford to ignore its impact. AI is reshaping the industry, offering unprecedented efficiency, personalization, and prediction capabilities. But what exactly is AI in the context of marketing, and how can we harness it to its full potential?

AI Demystified in Marketing Context

First off, let's define AI in simpler terms. In marketing, AI refers to technology that mimics human intelligence to perform tasks such as analyzing customer data, predicting trends, and automating repetitive activities. It encompasses machine learning, natural language processing (NLP), and other advanced algorithms designed to understand and anticipate consumer behavior.

Understanding AI begins with appreciating its ability to process vast amounts of data. Traditional marketing might rely on surveys and focus groups to gather insights, but AI can analyze millions of data points in seconds. This allows marketing teams to make data-driven decisions rapidly, rather than relying on outdated or anecdotal evidence.

The Building Blocks of AI in Marketing

At the heart of AI are algorithms—special sets of instructions programmed to solve specific problems. These algorithms continually learn from new data, improving their accuracy over time. Machine learning, a subset of AI, involves training these algorithms to identify patterns and make predictions based on data inputs. This capability is pivotal for personalized marketing strategies.

Imagine having an assistant that learns from every campaign you run. It evaluates what worked and what didn't, then refines future strategies accordingly. That's AI in a nutshell. It's like having a tireless, constantly improving teammate who's always on the lookout for ways to optimize your marketing efforts.

The Benefits of AI in Marketing

There are numerous benefits to integrating AI into your marketing toolkit. Here are a few worth considering:

- **Efficiency:** AI can automate routine tasks, freeing up your team to focus on more strategic activities. Think content scheduling, customer segmentation, and even ad placement.

- **Personalization:** AI enables one-to-one marketing at scale. By analyzing data from various touchpoints, it can customize messages and offers for individual consumers, increasing engagement and conversion rates.

- **Prediction:** Predictive analytics driven by AI can forecast future trends and consumer behavior, allowing marketers to stay ahead of the curve.

- **Data Analysis:** AI's data processing capabilities make it possible to analyze massive datasets accurately and quickly, giving marketers deeper insights than ever before.

- **Optimization:** AI can continually test and refine marketing strategies, ensuring that campaigns perform at their best.

Efficiency, customization, and foresight are no longer luxuries; they are necessities in today's competitive market.

Real-World Applications: A Glimpse into the Future

Let's explore some real-world applications of AI in marketing. Take, for example, personalized email campaigns. Traditional campaigns might segment audiences into broad categories, but AI can tailor messages to individual preferences and behaviors, making each email relevant and engaging. This level of personalization significantly boosts open and click-through rates.

Consider chatbots—another AI marvel. These virtual assistants are available 24/7, providing instant customer service and support. They can handle common queries, freeing up human agents for more complex issues. More than that, chatbots can gather invaluable data on customer interactions and preferences, enriching your marketing insights.

Social media marketing is another arena where AI shines. It can analyze user interactions to identify the best times to post, the most engaging content types, and the optimal frequency of posts. Brands can leverage these insights to improve their social media strategies, ensuring that their content resonates with their audience.

AI's Role in Data-Driven Decision Making

Data is the lifeblood of modern marketing, and AI is the engine that drives data analysis and decision-making. No longer do marketers have to wade through spreadsheets or sift through mountains of data manually. AI tools can handle these tasks with remarkable speed and accuracy, providing actionable insights that guide marketing strategies.

For instance, AI-powered analytics tools can track customer journeys across multiple channels, providing a holistic view of customer interactions with a brand. These insights help marketers understand which touchpoints are most effective and how to allocate their resources for maximum impact.

Ethics and AI: A Balanced Approach

As powerful as AI is, it's crucial to approach it with a balanced perspective. Ethical considerations should be at the forefront of any AI implementation. Concerns about data privacy, transparency, and bias must be addressed to build trust with consumers and ensure that AI-driven marketing practices are fair and responsible.

Marketers need to be transparent about how they're using AI and consumer data. This includes informing customers about data collection practices and giving them control over their data. Additionally, it's essential to ensure that AI algorithms are free from biases that could skew results and harm certain groups.

The responsible use of AI in marketing is not just a moral imperative; it's a business necessity. Brands that prioritize ethical AI practices are more likely to build customer trust and loyalty, which are critical for long-term success.

Conclusion: Embracing the AI-Driven Future

As we wrap up this exploration of AI in marketing, it's clear that this technology offers tremendous potential for transforming the industry. From automating routine tasks to providing deep insights and driving personalization, AI is a powerful tool for marketers. However, like any tool, its effectiveness depends on how it's used.

Marketing professionals who embrace AI and learn to leverage its capabilities will be well-positioned to navigate the complexities of today's digital landscape. By understanding the fundamentals of AI, staying informed about the latest developments, and prioritizing ethical considerations, you can harness AI to create more effective, engaging, and responsible marketing strategies.

Ready to delve deeper? In the next chapter, we'll explore how marketing has evolved with AI and what this means for the future of the industry. Stay tuned!

CHAPTER 2:
THE EVOLUTION OF
MARKETING WITH AI

W e've explored the fundamental concepts of AI in marketing in the previous chapter. Now, it's time to delve into how this technology is revolutionizing the marketing landscape. Over the past few years, artificial intelligence has transitioned from a futuristic notion to a vital component of successful marketing strategies. This transformation hasn't occurred overnight—it's been a gradual evolution shaped by advancements in technology, data availability, and changing consumer behaviors.

The earliest instances of AI in marketing can be traced back to the development of machine learning algorithms designed to optimize ad placements and bidding strategies. These early tools provided a glimpse of AI's potential by automating processes that were previously manual and time-consuming. As machine learning capabilities expanded, so did their applicability in marketing. Businesses started to realize that AI could offer more than just automation; it could provide valuable insights and optimize the entire marketing funnel from awareness to conversion.

One of the most significant milestones in the evolution of AI in marketing was the rise of data analytics. With the explosion of digital data, marketers found themselves sitting on a goldmine of information. However, deriving actionable insights from this data was a challenge. AI stepped in to fill this gap. By leveraging algorithms that can analyze large datasets quickly and accurately, marketers began to uncover patterns and trends that were previously invisible. This marked the beginning of data-driven marketing—an approach that centers on using data to make more informed decisions about marketing strategies and tactics.

As AI continued to evolve, so did its applications in marketing. Predictive analytics emerged as a powerful tool, allowing marketers to forecast customer behavior and market trends with a high degree of accuracy. Predictive models, powered by AI, could analyze historical data to identify patterns and predict future outcomes. This capability transformed marketing from a reactive to a proactive discipline. Marketers could now anticipate customer needs, optimize their marketing campaigns, and allocate resources more effectively.

Personalization is another area where AI has had a profound impact. Consumers today expect personalized experiences across all touchpoints, and AI has enabled marketers to meet these expectations at scale. By analyzing customer data, AI can create highly targeted and individualized marketing messages. This goes beyond simply addressing a customer by their first name in an email. AI-driven personalization involves understanding a customer's preferences, behavior, and purchase history to deliver relevant content, product recommendations, and offers. The result is a more engaging and satisfying customer experience, which can lead to increased loyalty and higher conversion rates.

The integration of AI in marketing has also paved the way for more sophisticated customer segmentation. Traditional segmentation methods often relied on broad demographic categories that didn't capture the nuances of consumer behavior. AI, on the other hand, can analyze vast amounts of data to identify micro-segments based on behavioral, psychographic, and transactional attributes. This level of granularity allows marketers to tailor their strategies to different cus-

AI Marketing Mastery

tomer segments more effectively, resulting in higher engagement and better ROI.

Automation is another key aspect of AI's evolution in marketing. AI-powered tools have streamlined various marketing processes, from content creation to campaign management and analytics. For example, AI can automate repetitive tasks such as scheduling social media posts, sending out email campaigns, and generating reports. This not only saves time but also reduces the risk of human error. Moreover, AI can optimize these processes by continuously learning and improving from data, leading to more efficient and effective marketing operations.

AI's role in marketing is not limited to digital channels. It has also transformed traditional marketing methods. For instance, AI can enhance direct mail campaigns by predicting which customers are most likely to respond based on their past behavior and preferences. It can also improve in-store experiences by providing personalized recommendations and assistance through AI-powered kiosks and mobile apps. This integration of AI across both digital and physical touchpoints creates a seamless and cohesive customer journey.

Another critical development in the evolution of AI in marketing is the advent of conversational AI. Chatbots and virtual assistants have become increasingly popular tools for customer engagement. These AI-driven interfaces can handle a wide range of interactions, from answering frequently asked questions to assisting with purchases and resolving issues. By providing instant and accurate responses, chatbots enhance customer satisfaction and free up human agents to focus on more complex tasks. Furthermore, conversational AI can gather valuable data on customer preferences and behavior, which can be used to refine marketing strategies.

The adoption of AI in marketing has also led to more effective and efficient advertising. Programmatic advertising, which uses AI to automate the buying and selling of ad space, has revolutionized the advertising industry. AI algorithms can analyze real-time data to determine the best times, channels, and formats for displaying ads. This results in more precise targeting, higher engagement rates, and better ROI. Additionally, AI can optimize ad creative by testing different variations and identifying the most effective ones. This data-driven approach to advertising ensures that marketing budgets are used more effectively and efficiently.

As AI continues to evolve, its impact on marketing is only expected to grow. Emerging technologies such as natural language processing (NLP) and computer vision are opening up new possibilities for AI-driven marketing. NLP allows AI to understand and interpret human language more accurately, enabling more sophisticated interactions and content generation. Computer vision, on the other hand, can analyze visual content such as images and videos, providing valuable insights into consumer preferences and behavior. These advancements will further enhance the capabilities of AI in marketing, leading to more innovative and effective strategies.

The journey of AI in marketing is a continuous one, characterized by rapid advancements and ever-expanding possibilities. However, it's important to remember that the successful implementation of AI in marketing requires a strategic approach. Marketers need to stay informed about the latest developments, invest in the right tools and technologies, and continuously evaluate and refine their strategies. By embracing AI and leveraging its full potential, marketers can stay ahead of the competition and achieve sustainable growth.

Looking Ahead

In conclusion, the evolution of marketing with AI is a testament to the transformative power of technology. From automation and data analytics to personalization and predictive modeling, AI has revolutionized how marketers engage with consumers and drive business outcomes. As we look to the future, the potential of AI in marketing is boundless. By staying agile and innovative, marketers can harness the power of AI to create more meaningful and impactful connections with their audience.

In the next chapter, we'll explore how data-driven insights are at the heart of AI-powered marketing strategies. We'll delve into the various ways data can be leveraged to uncover valuable insights, inform decision-making, and drive marketing success.

CHAPTER 3:
DATA-DRIVEN INSIGHTS

In today's marketing landscape, the term "data-driven" appears almost as frequently as "innovative." Indeed, marketers leverage data like never before. Yet, it isn't merely the volume of data that matters but how we parse and utilize it to extract meaningful insights. That's where AI steps in, transforming raw data into actionable intelligence, ready to drive smarter decisions.

Marketing professionals, let's delve into the potential of data-driven insights powered by AI. This isn't just about crunching numbers; it's about understanding and predicting behaviors to craft targeted strategies that hit their mark. With the overwhelming amount of data flooding in from various channels, navigating through it can feel like trying to find a needle in a haystack. Fortunately, AI-powered tools can handle this immense task with ease, uncovering patterns and identifying trends that human eyes might miss.

The predictive power of AI is, quite frankly, game-changing. Imagine knowing what your customer might want before they do. This isn't magic; it's predictive analytics at work. By analyzing past behaviors, AI can forecast future actions, offering recommendations on product development, optimal pricing strategies, and personalized marketing tactics.

Consider a scenario where your AI system processes customer data to predict the best time to send a promotional email. Instead of a blanket approach, each customer receives communication exactly when they're most likely to engage. The result? Increased open rates, higher conversion rates, and a marketing campaign that feels personalized, even though it's powered by algorithms.

AI does more than just predict; it also uncovers surprising insights hidden deep within your data. This can lead to data-driven decisions that challenge conventional wisdom and foster innovation. For example, by analyzing customer purchase patterns, you might discover that a seemingly unpopular product surges in sales during a specific season or in a particular region. These nuanced insights can lead to targeted campaigns that capitalize on these trends.

Integrating AI into your marketing strategy also means empowering your team with real-time data. Gone are the days of waiting for quarterly reports to understand performance. With AI tools, you have a dynamic dashboard offering live updates on key metrics. This continuous feedback loop allows for agile decision-making, adapting strategies on the fly to optimize outcomes.

Now, let's address an important aspect — the visualization of data. While raw numbers can provide insights, visual representation can turn complex data sets into easily digestible formats. AI excels in generating intuitive dashboards, charts, and graphs that highlight critical metrics and trends. This not only boosts comprehension but also enhances strategic discussions, ensuring everyone in the team is on the same page.

However, harnessing data-driven insights isn't just about having the right AI tools; it's about asking the right questions. What are you looking to achieve? Are you aiming to improve customer retention or increase your conversion rate? The clarity of your objectives will guide the AI's focus, ensuring the insights you receive are aligned with your goals. Without this direction, even the most sophisticated AI can feel like a blunt instrument.

It's also crucial to maintain a balance between data and intuition. Yes, data-driven insights are invaluable, but they should complement rather than replace human creativity and instinct. The best marketing strategies are those that blend empirical evidence with the nuanced understanding that only professionals can provide.

Consider the competitive edge that comes with a data-informed strategy. When you understand your audience at a granular level, you can outmaneuver competitors by delivering precisely what people want, when they want it. This not only improves market positioning but also cultivates deeper customer loyalty.

So, how do you get started? Begin by ensuring that your data collection methods are robust and compliant with privacy standards. Quality data is the backbone of reliable insights. Utilize structured data from CRM systems and unstructured data from social media, surveys, and other touchpoints. Bringing these diverse data sets together offers a holistic view of your customer landscape.

Next, invest in the right AI tools and platforms that align with your business needs. Look for solutions that offer intuitive interfaces and robust analytics capabilities. Training your team on these tools is equally important; even the best technology will fall short if not utilized effectively.

Lastly, cultivate a data-driven culture within your organization. Encourage curiosity and critical thinking. Equip your team with the skills to interpret data and to ask challenging questions. Foster an environment where insights lead to iteration and improvement, rather than just validation of existing beliefs.

In conclusion, data-driven insights powered by AI are not just the future of marketing; they're the present. The ability to decode vast arrays of data and translate them into actionable strategies offers a formidable advantage. By embracing this approach, you're not just keeping pace with the evolving landscape; you're leading the charge. So, dive into your data, leverage AI's power, and watch your marketing efforts scale new heights.

CHAPTER 4:
CUSTOMER SEGMENTATION AND TARGETING

Imagine you're casting a fishing net. You aim to catch as many fish as you can, but if your net isn't designed to catch the type of fish you're targeting, you'll come up empty-handed. Marketing works much the same way. Without proper customer segmentation and targeting, your campaigns might not reach their full potential. AI presents a transformative opportunity to refine and revolutionize how we segment and target our audiences.

Customer segmentation involves dividing a broad consumer or business market, normally consisting of existing and potential customers, into sub-groups based on some type of shared characteristics. These characteristics can be geographical, demographic, psychographic, and behavioral, among others. AI enhances this process by identifying patterns and drawing insights from vast amounts of data that would be impossible for humans to process effectively.

The power of AI in customer segmentation lies in its ability to process and analyze large datasets quickly and accurately. Traditional methods of segmentation often relied on broad categories and assumptions that could miss key nuances. AI, on the other hand, uses machine learning algorithms to create more precise segments. These algorithms can analyze purchasing patterns, social media activity, online browsing behaviors, and even individual preferences observed in real-time.

One key advantage of AI-driven customer segmentation is the granularity it offers. Rather than lumping customers into broad categories, AI can create micro-segments. These are highly specific groups that share several nuanced traits. For instance, instead of targeting all male customers aged 25-34 with an interest in fitness, AI could help identify a segment of males in that age group who have purchased protein supplements in the last month, follow multiple fitness influencers on social media, and frequently search for home workout routines.

Effective customer segmentation empowers businesses to move beyond generic marketing strategies. Once refined segments are identified, targeted marketing campaigns can be developed to address the unique preferences and needs of these groups. In essence, your marketing message becomes more personalized, relevant, and appealing, significantly improving customer engagement and conversion rates.

Additionally, real-time data processing capabilities of AI mean that customer segments can be dynamically updated. As customer behaviors and preferences shift, AI algorithms can quickly reanalyze data and adjust segments accordingly. This ensures that marketing efforts remain relevant and resonant, maximizing the chances of success in an ever-evolving market landscape.

Now, let's turn our attention to targeting. The goal of targeting is to tailor your marketing efforts to appeal to the specific segments identified during the segmentation process. AI aids in this by predicting which marketing actions will be most effective for different segments and even individual customers. It's like having a crystal ball that shows you the best way to reach your audience.

For example, predictive analytics can forecast which products a customer is most likely to purchase based on their browsing history, past purchases, and even broader market trends. AI can predict the right time to send a marketing message, the channel to use (email, social media, direct mail, etc.), and the type of content that will most likely prompt a positive response. Simply put, AI takes the guesswork out of marketing.

Consider the case of email marketing. Traditional email campaigns might send the same message to thousands of recipients, but AI-driven targeting ensures each recipient receives content tailored to their specific needs and preferences. The result? Higher open rates, improved click-through rates, and ultimately, more conversions.

AI's role in social media targeting can't be understated either. Platforms like Facebook and Instagram offer advertisers sophisticated tools for targeting users based on myriad data points, from demographics and interests to behaviors and connections. Machine learning models analyze this data and help marketers create highly targeted ads that deliver better ROI.

Behavioral targeting, fueled by AI, takes this a step further. By analyzing user behavior on websites, AI can determine what an individual is interested in and serve ads or content that is highly relevant. This could be something as subtle as showing a customer an ad for hiking boots after they've spent considerable time reading about mountain trails and outdoor activities.

Another groundbreaking innovation is the use of AI in programmatic advertising, which automates the buying of ad space. AI algorithms can identify the best sites and times to place ads, who to target, and even adjust bids in real-time to optimize campaign performance. This level of automation and precision is changing the face of digital advertising, making it more efficient and effective.

The Impacts on ROI

By now, it's clear that AI-driven customer segmentation and targeting can profoundly impact your marketing ROI. When messages are both relevant and timely, they're more likely to resonate with your audience, leading to higher engagement and conversion rates. But how do you measure these improvements?

AI itself offers robust analytics tools that can track and report on various performance metrics. You can monitor which segments are performing well, which messages and channels are most effective, and where adjustments may be needed. These insights allow you to continually refine your strategies for even better results over time.

Ethical Considerations

As with any powerful tool, the use of AI in customer segmentation and targeting raises ethical considerations. Privacy is a significant concern, and businesses must ensure they're using customer data responsibly. Transparency about data usage, obtaining proper consent, and adhering to data protection regulations are non-negotiable. AI should be a tool for enhancing customer experience, not exploiting it.

Additionally, there's a risk of over-segmentation, where groups become too narrowly defined, resulting in marketing messages that feel invasive rather than helpful. Striking the right balance is essential to maintain customer trust and build long-term relationships.

The Road Ahead

The future of customer segmentation and targeting is undeniably exciting. With AI's continual advancement, we can expect even more sophisticated techniques to emerge. Augmented reality, voice search, and other technologies will likely play increasingly important roles in how we understand and engage with our customers.

Ultimately, the goal is to create a seamless and personalized customer experience. AI enables us to understand our customers deeply and reach them in ways that resonate on a personal level. But remember, technology is a means to an end. It's the human element—creativity, empathy, and ethical considerations—that will make your AI-driven marketing truly successful.

As you leverage AI for customer segmentation and targeting, keep refining, keep testing, and most importantly, keep the customer at the heart of your strategy. It's not just about being more efficient or effective; it's about making genuine connections that foster loyalty and drive long-term success.

Chapter 5:
Personalization and Customer
Experience

Personalization has emerged as a pivotal factor in delivering exceptional customer experiences in today's competitive market. By leveraging AI, marketers can craft highly personalized interactions that resonate deeply with consumers' preferences and behaviors. This not only elevates engagement but also fosters strong brand loyalty. Imagine a world where every touchpoint, from emails to product recommendations, feels uniquely tailored to each customer. AI makes this vision a reality by analyzing vast datasets to uncover insights into individual customer journeys. This data-driven approach translates into marketing strategies that are not just reactive but proactively anticipate needs. Ultimately, the goal isn't just to sell more but to enrich each customer's experience, making every interaction meaningful and relevant. As we explore advanced personalization techniques and the metrics for measuring success in the upcoming sections, keep in mind that the heart of personalization lies in understanding and valuing the customer's unique story.

Chapter 5.1: Advanced Personalization Techniques

In an ever-competitive marketplace, providing a unique and engaging customer experience is more critical than ever. To achieve this, advanced personalization techniques powered by artificial intelligence (AI) have become a game-changer. Personalization at scale goes beyond just addressing customers by their first names; it involves tailoring every interaction to meet their specific needs, preferences, and even moods. This transformation is driven by the ability of AI to analyze vast amounts of data and derive actionable insights in real-time.

One of the primary techniques in advanced personalization is the use of predictive analytics. By leveraging machine learning algorithms, marketers can predict future customer behaviors based on past interactions. For instance, if a customer repeatedly browses electronics but never purchases, predictive models can identify the barriers and recommend the right product at the optimal time. This level of foresight can significantly enhance conversion rates and boost customer loyalty.

Another powerful tool in personalization is dynamic content. Unlike static content that remains the same for all users, dynamic content changes based on the individual visitor's characteristics. AI enables this through content management systems that automatically serve different images, texts, and even layouts based on user data such as browsing history, demographic information, and real-time behavior. This ensures that each visitor gets a tailored experience that resonates with their unique preferences.

Personalized recommendations, particularly in e-commerce, have revolutionized how customers discover products. AI-driven recommendation engines analyze customer data to suggest items that align with their tastes and needs. These recommendations can be based on various factors, including previous purchases, browsing habits, and even what similar customers have bought. Companies like Amazon and Netflix have perfected this technique, leading to significant increases in sales and customer retention.

AI doesn't just enhance personalization for e-commerce; it also plays a significant role in content personalization. By analyzing user data, AI can determine which types of content engage particular segments of the audience. This ensures that marketing messages, blog posts, videos, and social media updates are aligned with the interests and behaviors of different audience segments. This kind of targeted content delivery not only improves engagement but also fosters a deeper connection with the brand.

As personalization techniques become more advanced, the concept of real-time personalization has gained prominence. Real-time personalization involves altering the customer experience on the fly, as the interaction is occurring. For example, an AI-driven system could change the homepage layout, recommend products, or offer special discounts in response to real-time cues from the customer's behavior. This can make the customer journey more fluid and intuitive, leading to higher satisfaction levels.

Sentiment analysis is another cutting-edge technique that feeds into advanced personalization. By analyzing customer reviews, social media posts, and other forms of feedback, AI can gauge public sentiment toward a brand or product. This analysis can then inform personalized outreach strategies that are more empathetic and relevant. For instance, if a customer expresses dissatisfaction over social media, an AI system can prompt a timely and personalized response to address the issue and restore the customer's confidence in the brand.

Chatbots have also evolved, with advanced AI enabling them to offer highly personalized interactions. Modern chatbots can recall previous conversations, understand user intent, and even mimic human-like conversational nuances. This allows businesses to provide 24/7 personalized customer service without human intervention, making it both cost-effective and highly efficient. Advanced chatbots can also upsell and cross-sell based on the customer's browsing history and purchase behavior, seamlessly integrating into the sales funnel.

Another exciting frontier in advanced personalization is the use of *visual and voice search*. AI-powered visual search engines can analyze images uploaded by users and find products that match their visuals, thereby providing a highly personalized shopping experience. Similarly, voice search, powered by natural language processing, allows users to interact with devices in more intuitive ways. Marketers can leverage these technologies to offer personalized recommendations and content through voice-activated devices, creating a seamless multi-channel experience.

Hyper-personalization takes the idea of personalization a step further by customizing every possible aspect of the customer experience. This involves not only understanding what the customer likes but also when, where, and how they prefer to be engaged. AI can analyze data points such as location, time of day, and even the weather to determine the best time to send marketing messages or push notifications. This level of detail ensures that the interaction is contextually relevant, increasing the likelihood of user engagement.

Moreover, advanced personalization isn't just limited to digital interactions. AI-driven personalization can also enhance the in-store experience. For instance, using beacon technology, retailers can send personalized offers and recommendations to customers' smartphones while they are shopping in physical stores. By merging online and offline data, businesses can create a cohesive and personalized omnichannel experience that caters to the customer wherever they are.

In the realm of email marketing, advanced personalization techniques powered by AI can significantly amplify the impact of campaigns. Predictive analytics can determine the best time to send emails and the types of content that resonate most with the recipient. Furthermore, dynamic content within emails can be tailored to the recipient's behavior, preferences, and past purchases, making each email unique and highly relevant.

Social media platforms offer another fertile ground for advanced personalization. AI can analyze users' interactions on social media to deliver highly personalized ads and content. For example, social listening tools can track mentions and sentiments around specific topics, allowing brands to tailor their social media content to what their audience is currently interested in. This level of personalization can significantly improve engagement and brand loyalty.

However, it's important to approach advanced personalization with a balanced strategy. While AI provides unparalleled capabilities for personalizing the customer experience, it's crucial to maintain transparency and protect user privacy. Leveraging customer data must be done responsibly, adhering to data protection laws and ensuring that customers are aware of how their data is being used. Transparent data practices build trust and encourage customers to share more information, which in turn enhances the effectiveness of personalization efforts.

Finally, the implementation of these advanced personalization techniques requires ongoing testing and optimization. What works today may not work tomorrow, as customer behaviors and preferences are constantly evolving. AI can help by continuously analyzing interaction data and identifying patterns that indicate what's working and what's not. This allows marketers to make data-driven adjustments in real-time, ensuring that the personalization strategy remains effective and relevant.

In conclusion, advanced personalization techniques powered by AI offer marketers the tools to create unique, engaging, and memorable customer experiences. By understanding and predicting customer behaviors, delivering dynamic content, leveraging real-time personalization, and integrating omnichannel data, brands can not only meet but exceed customer expectations. However, the key to success lies in responsibly harnessing the power of AI, maintaining transparency, and continually optimizing strategies to stay ahead in the dynamic landscape of modern marketing.

Chapter 5.2: Measuring Personalization Success

Personalization is at the forefront of modern marketing, driven by AI's ability to tailor experiences to individual customers. However, the success of these personalized efforts must be measurable to justify the investment and optimize future strategies. In this section, we'll delve into the key metrics, tools, and methodologies needed to assess the impact of personalization on customer experience.

First, it's crucial to define what success means for your organization. For some, success might be increased customer retention, while others might aim for higher conversion rates or enhanced customer loyalty. Each business will have its own unique goals and KPIs (Key Performance Indicators) that paint the picture of success. Identifying which metrics are relevant is the first step in measuring personalization success.

One of the most straightforward metrics to look at is conversion rate. If a personalization strategy is effective, we'd expect to see a significant uptick in conversions. AI-driven personalization often adjusts content, product recommendations, and communication timing based on user behavior. Monitoring how these changes affect conversion rates can provide concrete evidence of success.

Customer engagement is another vital metric. Personalization should lead to more meaningful interactions with your brand. Engagement metrics such as click-through rates, time spent on site, and interaction with personalized content can give you a good sense of how well your personalization efforts are resonating with your audience.

Click-through rate (CTR)

Time spent on site

Interaction rate with personalized content

Repeat visits and frequency

Delving deeper, customer retention and loyalty become key indicators. Personalization efforts aim to make customers feel understood and valued, thereby increasing their likelihood of returning to do more business with you. Metrics here include repeat purchase rates, customer lifetime value (CLV), and subscription renewal rates. An increase in any of these metrics generally signals that your personalization strategies are effective.

Customer Lifetime Value (CLV): By providing a personalized experience, you encourage customers to engage more deeply with your brand, thereby extending their lifetime value. Monitoring CLV allows you to gauge the long-term impact of personalization on your revenue.

Beyond quantitative data, qualitative feedback from customers can provide nuanced insights into how well personalization efforts are working. Surveys, feedback forms, and customer interviews can help you understand if customers feel the impact of your personalization efforts and if it's meeting their expectations. Questions should be aligned with your KPIs to ensure you gather relevant data.

For instance, customer satisfaction scores (CSAT) and Net Promoter Scores (NPS) offer a snapshot of how customers perceive your personalized efforts. Through these, you can identify whether personalization is enhancing their overall experience and, importantly, where you need to make improvements.

Net Promoter Score (NPS)

Customer Satisfaction Score (CSAT)

Open-ended survey questions

Implementing A/B testing is another effective method to measure the success of your personalization strategies. A/B testing involves comparing the performance of personalized content and offers against non-personalized ones. This method provides clear, actionable data on what works best for your audience.

Another critical area for evaluation involves tracking customer journey analytics. By mapping customer interactions from first contact to conversion and beyond, you can identify which touchpoints are most influenced by personalization. Tools like omnichannel analytics and customer journey mapping software can offer a cohesive view of how customers interact with different elements of your personalized strategy.

It's also essential to leverage advanced AI algorithms that help in predictive analytics. These algorithms can forecast the potential success of personalization tactics by learning from past data and identifying patterns that humans might miss. By predicting which strategies are likely to succeed, you can proactively adjust your approaches to maximize impact.

Furthermore, ROI (Return on Investment) is an overarching metric that consolidates the effectiveness of personalization across various fronts. Calculating the ROI of personalization efforts involves more than just comparing revenue before and after implementation; it encompasses cost savings, customer lifetime value improvements, and enhanced brand loyalty. Comprehensive ROI analysis will highlight whether the resources invested in personalization are yielding the desired returns.

Continual assessment and adjustment are crucial. Personalized marketing isn't a one-time effort but a dynamic strategy that evolves based on real-time customer data. Regularly audit your metrics, analyze your results, and refine your strategies. AI tools can automate much of this analysis, providing real-time insights that allow for agile responses to changing customer behaviors.

There's a motivational aspect to all this as well. Measuring the success of personalization is not just about numbers; it's about creating an emotional connection with customers. When customers feel that a brand understands their needs and preferences, they're more likely to become advocates. This emotional connection is a powerful catalyst for long-term loyalty and growth.

Lastly, share your findings with your team. Transparent communication about what's working and what's not can foster a culture of continuous improvement. Engaging your team in the metrics and data fosters a sense of ownership and helps everyone stay aligned with the overall goal: delivering a superior customer experience through effective personalization.

In conclusion, measuring the success of personalization requires a balanced approach that includes quantitative metrics, qualitative insights, and predictive analytics. By focusing on relevant KPIs like conversion rates, customer engagement, retention, and ROI, and making use of advanced analytics tools, you can fine-tune your strategies for maximum impact. Remember, the ultimate aim is to forge an emotional bond with your customers, turning data points into meaningful relationships that enhance both customer satisfaction and business success.

CHAPTER 6:
AUTOMATED MARKETING CAMPAIGNS

In an ever-evolving digital landscape, the power of automated marketing campaigns can't be overstated. By leveraging sophisticated AI algorithms, marketers can create dynamic and adaptive campaigns that not only reach the right audience but also engage them in a highly personalized manner. Imagine being able to send perfectly timed emails, tailor social media posts to individual preferences, and launch high-impact advertising with minimal manual intervention. These automated systems continuously learn and optimize, ensuring that every touchpoint is as effective as possible, ultimately driving higher conversion rates and customer satisfaction. The magic lies in the seamless integration of AI-powered tools that make complex tasks effortless, freeing up valuable time for marketers to focus on strategy and creativity. Embrace the potential of AI-driven automation and transform your marketing endeavors into finely-tuned, results-oriented campaigns.

Chapter 6.1: Email Marketing Automation

Email marketing has long been a cornerstone of digital marketing strategies. The introduction of automation into this realm has turned the tables, bringing about an unprecedented level of sophistication and efficiency. But, what exactly does email marketing automation entail? At its core, it refers to the use of software to automate the process of sending scheduled, personalized, and trigger-based emails to your audience. Such automation not only saves time but also enhances the effectiveness of your campaigns.

The allure of email marketing automation lies in its potential to deliver highly personalized experiences at scale. Imagine sending a welcome email series to new subscribers, birthday wishes on a customer's special day, or tailored product recommendations based on past behavior—all automatically. With AI-driven algorithms, these messages can become incredibly nuanced, taking into account a multitude of data points to craft the perfect email for each recipient.

One of the key advantages of email marketing automation is the ability to send trigger-based emails. These are automated emails that are sent when a specific event or behavior occurs, such as a customer abandoning their shopping cart or signing up for a newsletter. Utilizing triggers ensures timely and relevant communication, thereby increasing the likelihood of engagement and conversions.

For marketers, this means less time spent on manual tasks and more opportunities to focus on strategy and creativity. By automating repetitive tasks, you can channel more energy into crafting compelling content and building deeper relationships with your audience.

The first step in implementing email marketing automation is to choose the right platform. There are several available, each with its own strengths and weaknesses. Look for features that align with your specific needs, such as segmentation capabilities, A/B testing options, and detailed analytics. Also, consider the integration capabilities with your existing CRM system to ensure seamless data flow.

Segmentation is the foundation of effective email marketing automation. It involves dividing your email list into sub-groups based on specific criteria such as demographics, purchase history, and engagement levels. AI can analyze an enormous amount of data to identify patterns and trends, helping you create highly-targeted segments. Sending tailored messages to these segments can significantly boost open and click-through rates.

Moreover, AI-powered personalization goes beyond just addressing the recipient by name. It can tailor the entire email content, including product recommendations, subject lines, and call-to-action buttons, based on an individual's past behavior and preferences. Such granular personalization ensures that your emails resonate more deeply with your audience.

Once your segments and personalization strategies are in place, the next step is to design your automated email workflows. These are essentially the blueprint for your automated campaigns, outlining the sequence of emails that will be sent, the triggers that will initiate them, and the rules that govern their sending. For instance, a common workflow could involve sending a welcome email when someone subscribes, followed by a series of educational emails over the next few weeks.

An often overlooked but critical aspect of email marketing automation is the importance of testing and optimization. A/B testing allows you to experiment with different subject lines, email designs, and call-to-action buttons to determine what resonates best with your audience. Continual optimization based on these insights ensures that your campaigns are always improving and evolving to meet changing customer expectations.

analytics plays a crucial role in understanding the effectiveness of your email marketing automation efforts. Most platforms offer robust analytics tools that allow you to track key metrics such as open rates, click-through rates, conversion rates, and revenue generated. By analyzing this data, you can gain valuable insights into what's working and what's not, enabling you to make data-driven decisions to enhance your campaigns.

Real-time data analysis is another game-changer in this realm. With AI, you can monitor how subscribers interact with your emails and adjust your strategies on the fly. This level of agility is invaluable in today's fast-paced digital landscape, where customer preferences and behaviors can shift rapidly.

Additionally, one cannot underestimate the value of integrating email marketing automation with other marketing channels. Cross-channel marketing ensures a unified message and experience for your audience. For example, your email automation platform could sync with your social media management tools to follow up an email campaign with a targeted social ad. This multi-channel approach helps reinforce your messaging and keeps your brand top of mind.

Privacy and consent are becoming increasingly important in the world of email marketing. With regulations such as GDPR and CAN-SPAM, it's crucial to ensure that your email automation practices are compliant. AI can assist in managing consent records and providing options for easy opt-out. Respecting privacy not only keeps you compliant but also builds trust with your audience, fostering long-term relationships.

The transformative potential of AI in email marketing automation extends beyond operational efficiencies. It enables you to build more meaningful connections with your customers. By anticipating their needs and delivering valuable content at precisely the right moments, you make your brand a trusted advisor, not just a vendor.

Think about how far email marketing has come—from simple, one-size-fits-all newsletters to sophisticated, AI-driven campaigns that can predict what your customers want before they do. It's an evolution that's made email one of the most powerful tools in a marketer's arsenal.

Looking ahead, the future of email marketing automation holds even more promise. As AI technologies continue to evolve, the capabilities of automation platforms will only become more advanced. Predictive analytics, for instance, could soon enable marketers to not only react to customer behavior but to anticipate it, making email campaigns even more proactive and effective.

In summary, email marketing automation powered by AI is not just a time-saver, it's a game-changer. By leveraging advanced segmentation, personalization, and real-time analytics, you can deliver remarkably relevant content to your audience. The result? Higher engagement, increased conversions, and stronger customer loyalty. The tools and techniques are available—it's up to you to harness them and build the kind of email campaigns that not only reach your audience but truly resonate with them.

Chapter 6.2: Social Media Automation

In the dynamic landscape of automated marketing campaigns, social media automation stands as a game-changing element. The sheer volume of content shared across platforms like Facebook, Twitter, Instagram, LinkedIn, and others can be overwhelming. For marketing professionals, leveraging automation tools for social media can turn this potential chaos into a well-oiled machine that drives meaningful engagement and measurable results.

Automating social media posts saves time and ensures consistency. Imagine the ability to schedule posts weeks or even months in advance. This means that rather than scrambling to craft the perfect tweet or Instagram caption at the last minute, marketers can strategically plan and execute their social media content, ensuring it aligns with broader marketing campaigns and organizational objectives. But it goes beyond merely scheduling posts; it also encompasses analytics, audience insights, and even automated responses.

One of the most significant benefits of social media automation is the ability to maintain a consistent presence. Consistency in posting helps keep your audience engaged and shows that your brand is active and invested in communicating with its followers. Using tools like

Hootsuite, Buffer, or Sprout Social, marketers can prepare a month's worth of content in advance, giving them more time to focus on real-time engagement and creative tasks.

However, automation doesn't mean sacrificing quality for convenience. The key lies in finding the balance between automated posts and authentic, spontaneous interaction. While scheduled posts handle the routine, analytics from social media automation tools provide deeper insights into what resonates with your audience. These analytics can help refine content strategies, making future posts even more effective.

Another advantage is enhancing customer service. Through AI-powered bots and automated responses, brands can ensure that no customer query goes unanswered. Automation tools can categorize and prioritize incoming messages, directing them to the appropriate department or responding with pre-written replies. This feature is particularly beneficial for handling FAQs, allowing human representatives to focus on more complex issues.

Moreover, social media automation tools help with data collection and analysis. These tools offer comprehensive insights into audience behavior, engagement metrics, and performance trends. With this data, marketers can make informed decisions, tweak campaigns in real-time, and allocate resources more efficiently. Insights derived from these analytics can guide everything from the best times to post to the types of content that generate the most engagement.

But with all these advantages, there's a common pitfall to be wary of: sounding robotic. Automated posts, when not done correctly, can come off as impersonal and disconnected. Therefore, it's essential to add a human touch. This can be achieved through personalized responses, engaging stories, and even real-time interactions. The goal is to use automation to handle the mundane while freeing up time for genuine, creative interaction with your audience.

Integration with other marketing tools amplifies the power of social media automation. By connecting social media tools with CRM systems, email marketing platforms, or even e-commerce sites, you create a cohesive marketing ecosystem. This integration allows for a seamless flow of data, ensuring that your message is consistent across all channels and touchpoints. For instance, a customer who engages with a social media post may receive a follow-up email with personalized content, bridging the gap between different marketing platforms.

Understanding the nuances of each social platform is also crucial. Each platform has its own set of best practices, audience demographics, and content types that perform well. For example, Instagram favors visual content, Twitter thrives on timely updates and trending hashtags, while LinkedIn is the go-to for professional insights and networking. Tailoring your automated posts to fit the unique dynamics of each platform can significantly enhance their effectiveness.

It's also worth exploring advanced features like A/B testing within social media automation tools. By testing different variations of a post, marketers can determine which version performs better before fully rolling it out. This technique can optimize engagement and reach, ensuring that campaigns are as effective as possible.

On the flip side, marketers must remain vigilant about monitoring the automated efforts. Automation doesn't imply setting and forgetting. Regular checks and updates are essential to ensure everything is functioning as intended. This includes verifying that posts are being published correctly, links are working, and that engagement is being monitored effectively. A hands-on approach ensures that automation complements your marketing efforts rather than controlling them.

With the rapid advancements in AI, the future of social media automation holds even more promise. Technologies like natural language processing (NLP) and machine learning are becoming increasingly sophisticated, allowing for more personalized and contextually relevant interactions. As these technologies evolve, they will enable even more seamless and efficient automation, offering insights and capabilities that were previously unimaginable.

Yet, the human element remains irreplaceable. AI and automation are tools to enhance human efforts, not replace them. Success in social media automation lies in the synergy between advanced technology and human creativity and empathy. By harnessing the strengths of both, marketers can create campaigns that are not only efficient but also genuinely engaging and impactful.

In conclusion, social media automation is a powerful ally in the realm of automated marketing campaigns. It offers numerous benefits, from saving time and maintaining consistency to providing deep insights and enhancing customer service. However, the key to success lies in balancing automation with human touch, leveraging data insights, and continuously optimizing efforts. As we embrace the future of AI in marketing, the combined power of automation and human creativity will undoubtedly unlock unprecedented opportunities for engagement and growth.

CHAPTER 7:
CHATBOTS AND CUSTOMER SERVICE

Chatbots have revolutionized the way businesses interact with their customers. By leveraging artificial intelligence, chatbots provide instant responses, handle multiple inquiries simultaneously, and operate around the clock. This chapter delves into how chatbots can drastically improve customer service and transform the customer journey.

Initially, chatbots were simple rule-based programs that could only handle a limited set of predefined responses. They answered basic, frequently asked questions (FAQs) and performed straightforward tasks. Over time, advancements in natural language processing (NLP) and machine learning (ML) have significantly enhanced their capabilities. Modern chatbots can understand context, learn from interactions, and provide responses that mimic human conversation.

One of the standout benefits of chatbots is their strategic advantage in delivering customer service. Imagine a customer visiting a website outside of business hours. Without a chatbot, that customer's query would go unanswered until the next business day, potentially leading them to seek solutions elsewhere. A chatbot, on the other hand, can engage the customer immediately, providing the information they need or even guiding them through complex processes.

These bots can handle an enormous volume of inquiries simultaneously—something human agents simply can't achieve. This means that during peak times, such as product launches or promotional events, chatbots can ensure that all customers receive timely responses without overwhelming human call centers. By managing routine queries, chatbots free up human agents to focus on more complex and sensitive issues, enhancing overall efficiency and customer satisfaction.

Another transformative aspect is personalization. While we will tackle advanced personalization techniques and metrics in other parts of this book, chatbots play a critical role here as well. They can customize their responses based on user data, recommend products based on browsing history, and even remember past interactions to provide a seamless experience. This level of personalization drives engagement and enhances the customer experience, making each interaction feel unique and valued.

Implementing a chatbot requires careful planning and execution. Start with defining clear objectives: What tasks should the chatbot perform? What are the key performance indicators (KPIs) for its success? Once the objectives are set, the next step is to select the appropriate platform or tool. Various options are available, from simple, plug-and-play bots to more sophisticated solutions requiring some degree of programming and customization.

When designing the bot's conversation flow, simplicity and clarity are paramount. Users should be able to interact with the chatbot without feeling confused or frustrated. Incorporating NLP can greatly enhance the chatbot's ability to understand and respond to diverse inputs, but it's crucial to ensure that the bot can recognize when to escalate inquiries to human agents. A seamless hand-off process maintains the quality of service and avoids customer frustration.

Integration with existing systems is another critical aspect. For a chatbot to provide accurate, personalized responses, it must have access to relevant data, whether that's customer databases, product inventories, or CRM systems. This ensures that the chatbot doesn't just provide generic responses but pulls from real-time data to offer actionable insights and solutions.

As chatbots continue to evolve, their applications in customer service become increasingly diverse. For instance, they are being used for lead generation and qualification. A chatbot can ask visitors initial questions to determine their needs and direct qualified leads to the sales team. This not only improves the efficiency of the sales process but also enhances the customer journey by ensuring that inquiries are addressed promptly.

Moreover, automated chatbots are making strides in multilingual support. Handling customer inquiries in various languages opens up new markets and provides an inclusive environment for users from different backgrounds. NLP algorithms have advanced to the point where chatbots can understand and translate multiple languages, ensuring a broader reach for businesses.

The impact of chatbots on metrics like customer satisfaction (CSAT) and Net Promoter Score (NPS) is noteworthy. Quick response times, efficient resolution of issues, and personalized interactions can significantly improve these metrics. Monitoring these KPIs provides invaluable insights into how well the chatbot is performing and where it needs improvements.

Security and privacy are also critical considerations in implementing chatbots. They often interact with sensitive customer information, from payment details to personal data. Ensuring that these interactions are secure and comply with data protection regulations is non-negotiable. Encryption, secure data storage, and compliance with laws like the GDPR are essential to maintain trust and protect customer information.

The future of chatbots in customer service looks incredibly promising. With advancements in artificial general intelligence (AGI), we can anticipate even more sophisticated bots capable of handling intricate queries with ease. They may also integrate with other AI systems to offer predictive support—identifying potential issues before they arise and offering proactive solutions to enhance the user experience.

The success stories are myriad. For example, a leading e-commerce platform implemented a chatbot that reduced their average response time by 70% and increased customer satisfaction scores by 15%. Another case involves a healthcare provider whose chatbot significantly streamlined the appointment scheduling process, freeing up human resources for more patient-centric activities.

It's not just about efficiency and speed; chatbots also gather crucial data. Every interaction is an opportunity to learn more about customers—what they want, what problems they face, and how they prefer to interact. This data can be analyzed to refine marketing strategies, develop new products, and enhance service offerings.

In conclusion, chatbots are not just a technological novelty; they are a strategic asset in the modern business landscape. By integrating chatbots into your customer service framework, you can offer timely, efficient, and personalized support that meets and exceeds customer expectations. As technology continues to evolve, the capabilities and applications of chatbots will only expand, offering even more opportunities for businesses to enhance their customer service and overall engagement strategies.

Next, we'll explore the fascinating world of predictive analytics, uncovering how AI can help foresee trends, behaviors, and needs before they even occur.

CHAPTER 8:
PREDICTIVE ANALYTICS

Predictive analytics is revolutionizing the way marketing professionals engage with their audiences. By harnessing data, algorithms, and machine learning models, predictive analytics enables marketers to anticipate future behaviors, trends, and outcomes. It shifts the marketing approach from being reactive to proactive, allowing businesses to not only understand what happened but also to foresee what will happen. In this chapter, we'll explore how predictive analytics is transforming marketing, the methodologies behind it, and practical applications you can integrate into your strategies.

The cornerstone of predictive analytics lies in collecting and analyzing vast amounts of data. This data can come from various sources such as customer interactions, sales records, social media activity, and more. The key is to have clean, structured, and relevant data. Once this data is prepared, sophisticated algorithms analyze it to identify patterns and correlations that aren't immediately obvious to the human eye.

One of the primary benefits of predictive analytics is its ability to provide insights into customer behavior. For example, by examining historical purchasing patterns, a predictive model can forecast future purchases. This allows marketers to tailor their campaigns more accurately, targeting customers with products and offers they are more likely to respond to. It's a game changer for personalized marketing.

Another critical application of predictive analytics is in customer retention. Predictive models can identify which customers are most likely to churn based on their behavior and interaction history. With this foresight, businesses can implement timely interventions such as personalized offers or targeted communication to retain these customers. It saves costs associated with acquiring new customers and enhances customer loyalty.

A keyword in predictive analytics is "segmentation." By segmenting customers into various clusters based on predictive models, marketers can tailor their strategies to each group's needs and preferences. For example, a retailer might segment customers based on their predicted lifetime value. High-value customers might receive exclusive offers, while those with lower predicted value could be nurtured through targeted content to increase their engagement.

Let's discuss the methodologies that make predictive analytics possible. One commonly used approach is regression analysis, which identifies relationships between dependent and independent variables. Another is classification, where algorithms are used to categorize or classify data points into predefined categories. Clustering is another method that groups data points based on their similarities, without predefined categories.

Machine learning plays a significant role in predictive analytics. Algorithms such as decision trees, neural networks, and support vector machines are commonly used. These models can learn from data and improve their predictions over time. Supervised learning algorithms are trained on labeled data, while unsupervised learning deals with unlabeled data and finds hidden patterns within it.

The integration of predictive analytics into marketing strategies requires collaboration between data scientists and marketing professionals. Data scientists bring technical expertise in building and fine-tuning models. Marketers, on the other hand, provide insights into customer behavior and marketing tactics. This synergy ensures that predictive models are not only accurate but also actionable.

The practical applications of predictive analytics in marketing are vast. For example, in email marketing, predictive models can determine the best time to send emails to each subscriber, based on their past interaction patterns. This becomes especially powerful when combined with personalized content, leading to higher open rates and conversions.

In digital advertising, predictive analytics can optimize ad targeting. By predicting which users are most likely to convert, advertisers can allocate their budgets more efficiently, reducing waste and maximizing ROI. This level of precision is invaluable in today's competitive landscape.

Financial forecasting is another area where predictive analytics shines. By analyzing past sales data and market trends, predictive models can forecast future revenue, helping businesses plan their budgets and resources more effectively. It adds a layer of certainty to an otherwise uncertain future.

Implementing predictive analytics isn't without its challenges. One of the main hurdles is data quality. Inaccurate, incomplete, or outdated data can lead to erroneous predictions, causing more harm than good. Therefore, maintaining high standards of data hygiene is paramount. Regular updates, validation, and cleaning processes are necessary to ensure the data's integrity.

Another challenge is the complexity of building and maintaining predictive models. It requires specialized knowledge and skills, which can be a barrier for many organizations. Investing in the right talent, whether through hiring or training existing employees, is essential for the successful adoption of predictive analytics.

Despite these challenges, the rewards of using predictive analytics in marketing are substantial. Companies that effectively leverage predictive analytics can achieve improved customer satisfaction, increased sales, and higher marketing efficiency. It allows them to stay ahead of the curve, anticipating market changes and consumer demands before they happen.

In conclusion, predictive analytics is a powerful tool that enables marketers to take a forward-looking approach. By leveraging the wealth of data available and applying sophisticated analytical techniques, it's possible to predict future trends and behaviors accurately. As AI and machine learning technologies continue to evolve, the potential of predictive analytics in marketing will only grow, offering new opportunities to innovate and excel.

As you continue on this journey of integrating AI into your marketing strategies, remember that predictive analytics is just one piece of the puzzle. It works best when combined with other AI-driven tools and techniques discussed in this book. The future of marketing is bright, and those who embrace predictive analytics will lead the way in creating engaging, personalized, and highly effective marketing campaigns.

CHAPTER 9:
AI-DRIVEN CONTENT CREATION

The world of content creation has seen transformative changes with the advent of artificial intelligence (AI). As marketing professionals, embracing these technological advancements is no longer optional—it's a necessity. AI can bring unprecedented efficiency and creativity to content generation, making it a cornerstone of modern marketing strategies.

So, what does AI-driven content creation entail? At its core, AI can generate text, images, and even videos based on data inputs and learned patterns. This means marketers can produce high-quality content faster and at scale. Whether it's blog posts, social media updates, or product descriptions, AI tools can speed up the process, allowing you to focus on strategy and creativity.

One of the most compelling advantages of AI in content creation is the ability to personalize content at a granular level. Traditional methods often fall short in delivering personalized messages to an extensive audience. With AI, you can analyze user data to tailor content that resonates with individual preferences, thus enhancing engagement and loyalty.

Consider, for instance, dynamic email newsletters. AI can tailor the content of each email based on a recipient's past interactions with your brand. This could be as simple as changing the product recommendations or as complex as adjusting the natural language tone to suit the recipient's personality. The outcome is a more engaged audience and improved conversion rates.

AI can also be a game-changer for social media content. Platforms like Facebook and Instagram are inundated with posts, making it challenging to stand out. AI can help craft compelling headlines, optimize post timing, and even suggest which types of content—videos, images, or text—are likely to perform best. All of these can significantly boost your social media metrics.

Additionally, AI tools like Natural Language Processing (NLP) and Natural Language Generation (NLG) are becoming increasingly sophisticated. NLP can analyze existing content to understand context, sentiment, and relevance, while NLG can generate human-like text based on this analysis. These technologies open doors to creating blog posts, reports, and even eBooks with minimal human intervention but maximal impact.

Content curation is another area where AI excels. With the overwhelming amount of information available today, curating relevant content for your audience can be a daunting task. AI can automate this process by aggregating, analyzing, and selecting high-quality content from a myriad of sources. This capability is especially useful for creating newsletters, industry reports, or social media content calendars.

But AI-driven content creation isn't limited to text. Tools like generative adversarial networks (GANs) are capable of producing high-quality images and videos. These can be used for everything from social media posts to advertising campaigns, providing an endless supply of creative assets. Imagine an e-commerce site where each product has a unique, AI-generated promotional video—seriously enhancing the customer experience.

However, AI-driven content creation isn't devoid of challenges. One of the main concerns is maintaining a consistent brand voice.

While AI can mimic human writing, it can sometimes lack the nuanced touch that only a human can provide. For this reason, it's crucial to integrate human oversight into your AI workflows. Think of AI as an assistant that handles the heavy lifting, allowing your creative team to focus on strategic and high-level tasks.

Moreover, AI-created content should always be vetted for accuracy and relevance. The technology can sometimes generate content that is off-brand or doesn't align with your business goals. Having a rigorous review process ensures that the content not only meets quality standards but also adheres to your brand guidelines.

Another consideration is ethical use of AI in content creation. Transparency is key; your audience should be aware that AI-generated content is part of your strategy. This builds trust and keeps your brand authentic. Ethical considerations also include ensuring that the data used for AI algorithms is sourced responsibly and respects user privacy.

Yet, the potential ROI from AI-driven content creation is immense. Not only can it streamline operations and reduce costs, but it can also foster deeper customer engagement and drive sales. The success metrics could range from higher click-through rates and conversion rates to improved time-on-site and reduced bounce rates.

To make the most out of these technologies, it's essential to choose the right AI tools for your needs. The market is flooded with various options, each offering unique features. Some of the popular tools include platforms like HubSpot's Content Strategy tool, Persado for crafting emotionally engaging messages, and Copy.ai for generating marketing copy. Evaluating these tools based on your specific requirements will enable you to integrate AI seamlessly into your content creation processes.

Continuous learning and adaptation are vital. AI technologies are evolving rapidly, and staying updated with the latest advancements will ensure that your marketing strategies remain ahead of the curve. Participating in industry forums, attending webinars, and engaging with thought leaders can provide valuable insights into emerging trends and best practices.

In summary, AI-driven content creation is revolutionizing the way marketers operate. It brings efficiency, personalization, and scalability to content production, allowing brands to connect with their audiences in more meaningful ways. While challenges exist, they are not insurmountable and can be effectively managed with the right approach. By integrating AI into your marketing strategy, you are not just keeping up with the competition; you are setting the stage for unparalleled success in your marketing endeavors.

The journey towards AI-driven content creation might seem daunting, but the rewards it promises are worth the effort. As you explore AI solutions, remember to keep the balance between automation and human creativity. This synergy will pave the way for innovative, impactful, and resonant marketing campaigns.

CHAPTER 10:
SEO AND AI

Search Engine Optimization (SEO) has always been a dynamic field influenced by technological advancements and algorithm updates. In recent years, the incorporation of artificial intelligence (AI) into SEO practices has revolutionized the way marketers and businesses approach online visibility. AI, with its ability to process enormous volumes of data and identify patterns, empowers marketers to optimize their content and strategies more effectively than ever before.

AI's role in SEO is multifaceted. From content creation to keyword research, AI-driven tools are enhancing every aspect of SEO. One of the primary ways AI is transforming SEO is through enhanced data analysis. Traditional keyword research methods, while effective, are labor-intensive and time-consuming. AI algorithms can analyze search patterns, user behavior, and competitors, offering insights that were previously unattainable. This deep analysis helps in identifying high-performing keywords and content gaps, enabling marketers to optimize their strategies with precision.

Moreover, user intent has become a significant focus in modern SEO, and AI plays a crucial role in understanding it. By leveraging machine learning and natural language processing (NLP), AI can interpret the context behind search queries. This allows marketers to create content that aligns more closely with what users are actually looking for, improving the chances of ranking higher in search results.

Next, let's dive into AI-powered content creation. Tools like GPT-3 and similar language models are capable of generating high-quality, relevant content that resonates with users. These tools analyze existing content on the web, learning from the best-performing articles and blogs to craft pieces that are not only engaging but also SEO-friendly. By producing content that matches user intent and adheres to SEO best practices, AI helps in driving organic traffic and improving search engine rankings.

Another significant advantage of AI in SEO is its application in predictive analysis and trend forecasting. AI can predict future trends based on historical data and current market scenarios. This allows businesses to stay ahead of their competition by adapting their SEO strategies preemptively. By knowing what your audience will be interested in tomorrow, you can create content today that meets future demands, ensuring continuous traffic and engagement.

Voice search optimization is an emerging trend that AI is assisting. With the rise of digital assistants like Alexa, Google Assistant, and Siri, optimizing for voice search has become essential. AI tools can help identify the differences between text and voice searches, focusing on the conversational nature of voice queries. This includes understanding natural language variations and local search patterns, enabling the creation of content that is both voice-search friendly and locally relevant.

Furthermore, AI tools are now capable of performing comprehensive audits of websites, identifying issues that could affect search engine rankings. These tools can detect technical SEO issues such as broken links, slow load times, and mobile-friendliness. By automatically flagging these issues, AI enables quicker resolutions, ensuring that websites remain optimized and user-friendly.

In addition to technical audits, AI can aid in the optimization of on-page elements. This includes optimizing meta tags, headers, and image alt texts. By analyzing what works for top-ranking pages, AI can suggest enhancements that align with best practices. These automated recommendations save time and ensure that all on-page elements contribute positively to SEO.

Link building, another critical component of SEO, also benefits from AI automation. AI can identify high-quality, relevant backlink opportunities by analyzing competitor backlinks and finding patterns. This strategic approach to link building enhances domain authority and boosts search engine rankings.

Let's not overlook the importance of local SEO, particularly for small businesses and brick-and-mortar stores. AI can optimize Google My Business listings by gathering data on user reviews, check-ins, and other local signals. This ensures that local businesses are more visible to potential customers in their vicinity.

AI also excels in competitor analysis. By monitoring competitors' SEO strategies, AI can provide insights into their strengths and weaknesses. This information helps in refining your own tactics, ensuring that you maintain a competitive edge. You can answer important questions such as: What keywords are they ranking for? What content is performing well for them? How is their backlink profile evolving?

In the ever-evolving landscape of SEO, staying updated with the latest algorithm changes is crucial. AI tools can monitor and analyze these updates in real-time, offering actionable insights to adapt your strategies accordingly. This proactive approach ensures that your SEO efforts remain effective despite frequent changes in search engine algorithms.

Additionally, AI enhances user experience (UX), which is increasingly tied to SEO performance. By analyzing user behavior on your site, AI can identify areas that need improvement, such as navigation, page layout, and content accessibility. Enhancing UX not only boosts user engagement and retention but also signals to search engines that your site provides value, thereby improving rankings.

Finally, the integration of AI and SEO demands a mindset shift. Marketers must embrace AI not just as a tool but as an integral part of their strategy. This involves continuous learning and adaptation, staying abreast of AI advancements, and being open to experimenting with new AI-driven tools and techniques. By adopting this approach, marketers can fully harness the power of AI to achieve their SEO goals and drive sustainable growth.

In conclusion, the synergy between SEO and AI offers immense potential for enhancing online visibility and driving organic traffic. By leveraging AI's capabilities in data analysis, content creation, predictive forecasting, and technical optimization, marketers can create more effective and efficient SEO strategies. As AI continues to evolve, staying ahead of the curve will require an agile approach, but the rewards of doing so are undeniable. Harness the power of AI in your SEO efforts, and watch your online presence soar to new heights.

CHAPTER 11:
AI IN ADVERTISING

As we delve into the transformative realm of AI in advertising, it's clear that artificial intelligence is revolutionizing how we connect with audiences and optimize ad spend. By utilizing AI, marketers can harness vast amounts of data to craft more targeted ad campaigns, reaching the right people at precisely the right time. This isn't just about automation—it's about intelligent decision-making, enabling unprecedented levels of personalization and efficiency. With AI, predictive algorithms can forecast consumer behaviors, optimize ad placements in real-time, and even generate creative content that resonates deeply with target demographics. The competitive edge AI provides is undeniable; it not only enhances ROI but also fosters deeper customer engagement and loyalty. Embracing AI in advertising means transitioning from traditional scattershot approaches to a laser-focused strategy that adapitates and evolves with market dynamics, setting the stage for sustained success and innovation in the digital advertising landscape.

Chapter 11.1: Programmatic Advertising

In today's dynamic marketing landscape, the role of programmatic advertising has never been more pivotal. Largely driven by advancements in artificial intelligence (AI), programmatic advertising allows for the automated buying and selling of ad inventory in real-time. This approach is revolutionizing how brands reach their target audiences, and it's vital for marketing professionals to grasp its potential fully.

At its core, programmatic advertising uses AI and machine learning algorithms to optimize the placement and timing of ads. This automation ensures that ads are shown to the right audience at the right time, based on data-driven insights and behavioral patterns. By leveraging vast amounts of data, AI helps marketers make more informed decisions, eliminating guesswork and reducing inefficiencies typically associated with traditional ad buying methods.

The biggest advantage of programmatic advertising is its scalability. What once required extensive manual input and negotiation can now be smoothly executed through automated platforms. This allows marketers to run numerous campaigns concurrently across multiple channels, optimizing each in real-time for better performance. Consequently, businesses can reach a broader audience with less effort and more precision, which translates to higher ROI.

Imagine you're about to launch a product targeted at tech-savvy millennials. With programmatic advertising, you can serve personalized ads to users who have shown interest in similar products or have relevant browsing behaviors. AI-driven algorithms pinpoint these users based on their activity across the web, ensuring your ad budget is spent efficiently. It's akin to having a sharp-shooter on your team, hitting the bullseye with each shot.

But it's not just about efficiency and precision. Programmatic advertising offers a more profound understanding of audience behavior. Real-time analytics and reporting provide insights into how and when audiences engage with ads, allowing for continuous optimization. When you understand what works and what doesn't, you can make adjustments on the fly, ensuring your campaigns remain relevant and performant.

To illustrate, consider a scenario where your current ad campaign isn't delivering the desired click-through rates. Programmatic platforms can rapidly analyze performance data and identify potential issues—be it the creative used, demographics targeted, or the timing of ad placements. With these insights, you can tweak various elements instantaneously and see the impact of those changes in real time. This agility is invaluable in a fast-paced digital landscape.

Furthermore, the integration of AI in programmatic advertising enhances creativity, too. Dynamic creative optimization (DCO) leverages AI to adjust ad creatives based on the viewer's profile and context. Imagine showing different ad versions to users depending on their location, browsing history, or even the weather. These kinds of personalized experiences are more engaging and can significantly improve conversion rates.

However, successful programmatic advertising isn't solely about automation and data. It also requires a strategic approach. Clear objectives, understanding your target audience, and continuously refining your tactics based on performance data are key to making the most of this technology. Without a strategic framework, even the most advanced tools can fail to deliver optimal results.

The landscape of programmatic advertising is continuously evolving, opening new frontiers for marketers. Innovations such as programmatic TV, audio, and out-of-home (OOH) ads are expanding the reach and capabilities of this technology. These advancements offer unparalleled opportunities for marketers to engage audiences across various touchpoints seamlessly.

While the benefits are substantial, it's crucial to address some challenges and considerations. Data privacy and ethical considerations are at the forefront. As with any AI-driven initiative, marketers must handle consumer data responsibly. Transparency in data usage and adherence to privacy regulations like GDPR and CCPA is essential to maintaining consumer trust and avoiding legal repercussions.

Equally important is the mitigation of ad fraud, which remains a significant concern in programmatic advertising. Employing robust fraud detection mechanisms and working with trusted platforms can minimize risks associated with fake clicks, bot traffic, and other fraudulent activities. Advanced AI systems are increasingly adept at identifying and mitigating such threats, ensuring your ad spend is protected.

Moreover, marketers need to remain agile and adaptable. The rapid pace of technological advancements means today's state-of-the-art solutions could become outdated tomorrow. Continuous learning and staying updated with industry trends are crucial for success in programmatic advertising. Engaging in professional development opportunities, participating in industry forums, and collaborating with tech-savvy professionals can ensure you stay ahead of the curve.

The marriage of AI and programmatic advertising represents a significant paradigm shift in how marketers approach campaign management. By harnessing the power of automation, data insights, and real-time optimization, marketers can achieve a level of precision and efficiency previously unattainable. This technological synergy not only drives superior marketing outcomes but also paves the way for more innovative and engaging consumer experiences.

To thrive in this new era, it's imperative for marketing professionals to embrace programmatic advertising whole-heartedly. This entails not just understanding the mechanics of AI and machine learning but also developing a strategic mindset geared towards continuous improvement and innovation. By doing so, you'll not only stay relevant but also set new standards in marketing excellence.

In conclusion, programmatic advertising stands as a testament to the transformative power of AI in marketing. It offers unprecedented opportunities for personalization, efficiency, and engagement. By adopting this technology thoughtfully and strategically, marketers can navigate the complexities of the digital ecosystem with confidence, delivering impactful and measurable results.

Chapter 11.2: Ad Targeting and Optimization

In an era where digital transformation is accelerating at a breakneck speed, AI-powered ad targeting has emerged as a crucial cornerstone for marketers aiming to maximize their advertising effectiveness. Through the use of advanced algorithms and data analytics, AI equips marketers with the ability to deliver highly personalized advertisements to specific audience segments. This is no longer a shot in the dark; it's a precise, laser-focused approach that optimizes both ad spend and engagement.

Gone are the days when advertisers relied solely on demographic data like age, gender, and location. Today, AI dives deep into psychographics, enabling a much more nuanced understanding of consumer behaviors and preferences. For instance, AI can analyze users' social media engagements, search history, and even purchase behavior to create a multi-faceted profile. This level of granularity facilitates hyper-targeted ad campaigns that resonate on a more personal level.

Let's talk a bit about contextual targeting. It's an approach where AI algorithms analyze the content that a user is currently engaging with to determine the most relevant ads to display. This technique mimics the human cognitive process, recognizing the context and sentiment behind the content. For marketers, this means ads are displayed in a more meaningful and less intrusive manner, aligning naturally with the user's current interests.

Another groundbreaking development is the rise of real-time bidding (RTB). RTB utilizes AI to make split-second decisions on ad placements based on continually updated data. It ensures that your ads are not just highly targeted but also dynamically optimized for performance. The convergence of AI and RTB means that your marketing efforts are always adapting, constantly fine-tuning to achieve the best possible results.

Moreover, AI-driven ad targeting doesn't just stop at online behavior analysis. It extends to offline data integration as well. By combining online and offline datasets, AI creates a holistic customer view, enabling cross-channel ad targeting. Imagine leveraging in-store purchase data to refine your online ad campaigns. The integration of these data streams allows for more robust and consistent targeting strategies.

One might wonder, how do we quantify the effectiveness of AI-powered ad targeting? Performance metrics are, of course, crucial. Click-through rates (CTR), conversion rates, and return on ad spend (ROAS) are some of the traditional metrics that can still offer valuable insights. However, AI introduces new dimensions to measurement, such as predictive analytics and sentiment analysis. Predictive analytics helps in forecasting the success of ad campaigns, which enables pre-emptive adjustments.

Additionally, AI can analyze consumer sentiment through natural language processing (NLP) to gauge how your audience is reacting to your ads. If sentiment analysis reveals a negative trend, the AI system can recommend or even autonomously implement changes to ad copy or targeting parameters, ensuring that your campaigns remain effective and relevant.

User privacy and ethical considerations are also paramount when discussing AI-driven ad targeting. As marketers, it's our responsibility to ensure that the data we collect and utilize complies with privacy laws such as GDPR and CCPA. AI can actually assist in this endeavor by automating compliance checks and ensuring that data usage is both ethical and lawful. In ethical AI, transparency is key. Consumers must be aware of how their data is being used and should have the option to opt-out if they choose.

Personalization has been a buzzword in marketing for a while, but AI takes it to another level. By continuously learning and adapting from new data inputs, AI-powered systems can offer truly personalized ad experiences that evolve over time. This dynamic personalization ensures that the ads remain relevant and engaging, thereby reducing ad fatigue among consumers.

Let's not forget the role of creative optimization in AI-targeted advertising. AI tools can analyze which types of creatives perform best across different segments and contexts. Based on this analysis, they can recommend or automatically generate variations of ad creatives to optimize performance. Imagine an AI system that can tweak your ad's visuals, copy, or call-to-action in real-time to better align with the audience's preferences and behaviors. This is no longer a futuristic concept; it's a current reality.

As we continue to pioneer new frontiers in ad targeting and optimization, collaboration between marketers and data scientists becomes increasingly vital. Marketers provide the strategic vision and understanding of consumer behavior, while data scientists bring quantitative skills and technical expertise. Together, this collaboration fuels the next wave of innovation in AI-driven advertising.

In summary, AI-powered ad targeting and optimization represent an unparalleled opportunity for marketers to elevate their advertising strategies. Through advanced data analytics, contextual and behavioral targeting, real-time bidding, and creative optimization, AI not only enhances the precision and relevance of ads but also drives better performance and ROI. As we navigate this transformative landscape, it's crucial to remain vigilant about privacy and ethics, ensuring that our strategies are both effective and respectful of consumer trust. It's not just about adopting AI; it's about integrating it thoughtfully and strategically into the fabric of our marketing endeavors.

CHAPTER 12:
INFLUENCER MARKETING WITH AI

A rtificial intelligence (AI) is revolutionizing countless industries, and marketing is no exception. One of the most dynamic areas of this transformation is influencer marketing. The use of AI in influencer marketing is opening up unprecedented opportunities for precision and effectiveness, enabling marketers to achieve results that were previously unimaginable.

To understand this better, let's first consider how influencer marketing works. Traditionally, it's about brands collaborating with individuals who have significant social media followings. These influencers can drive consumer behavior and create substantial brand awareness. But finding the right influencers, managing these relationships, and measuring the impact of campaigns can be quite challenging and resource-intensive.

This is where AI steps in. AI technologies provide solutions to these challenges, from identifying the perfect influencers to ensuring campaigns run smoothly and effectively. By analyzing vast amounts of data from social media platforms, AI can identify influencers who align perfectly with a brand's target audience, ensuring that marketing efforts are both efficient and effective.

The Role of AI in Influencer Identification

Finding the right influencer is critical. An influencer whose audience aligns with a brand's target demographic can significantly impact a campaign's success. AI algorithms can analyze millions of social media profiles to identify influencers whose followers match a brand's ideal customer profile. This not only saves time but also increases the effectiveness of influencer campaigns.

Consider the complexities involved: AI can analyze follower demographics, engagement rates, past brand collaborations, and sentiment around an influencer's content. These insights are invaluable. Traditional methods can barely scratch the surface compared to the depth of analysis that AI provides, making it a game-changer for modern marketing strategies.

Moreover, AI brings objectivity to the influencer selection process. Often, personal biases or subjective preferences can cloud decision-making, but AI-driven analytics ensures choices are data-backed and aligned with strategic goals. By reducing human error and subjectivity, brands can streamline their influencer marketing strategies and achieve better results.

Automation and Campaign Management

Once the right influencers are identified, managing campaigns is the next big hurdle. AI excels here by automating many of the repetitive and time-consuming tasks associated with influencer marketing. From outreach and contract management to content scheduling and performance tracking, AI tools can handle it all.

Outreach and Negotiation: AI can streamline the process of reaching out to influencers, negotiating terms, and finalizing collaborations. This reduces the manual effort required and speeds up the initiation of campaigns.

Content Scheduling: AI platforms can schedule influencer posts to go live at optimal times for maximum engagement. By analyzing historical data, AI determines the best times to publish content, ensuring campaigns achieve greater visibility.

Real-Time Monitoring: AI tools enable real-time monitoring of influencer campaigns. Brands can track engagement, conversions, and other relevant metrics as they happen, allowing for quick adjustments and more agile campaign management.

Through automation, brands can handle more complex campaigns with less effort, freeing up time to focus on creativity and strategy. AI-driven platforms also provide a centralized location for all campaign-related tasks, streamlining collaboration and making it easier for teams to stay organized.

Precision in Performance Measurement

One of the perennial challenges in marketing is measuring the return on investment (ROI) of campaigns. This is particularly tricky in influencer marketing, where the impact is often more qualitative than quantitative. AI offers sophisticated analytics tools that provide deeper insights into campaign performance.

These AI tools can track metrics such as engagement rates, click-through rates, and conversions. Additionally, they can perform sentiment analysis to understand the quality of the engagement—is the audience reacting positively, negatively, or neutrally? This level of detail allows marketers to judge the true impact of their campaigns and make data-driven decisions.

Moreover, AI can help in A/B testing different approaches to influencer marketing. By comparing the performance of various campaigns, brands can identify what works best and continually optimize their strategies. This iterative approach ensures that influencer marketing efforts remain effective and yield maximum results.

Ensuring Authenticity and Compliance

In recent years, authenticity has become a critical factor in influencer marketing. Audiences are quick to spot inauthentic endorsements, and brands that fail to maintain authenticity can suffer reputational damage. AI helps here too. By analyzing influencer content, AI can determine whether an influencer's posts align with their regular content and voice, ensuring that collaborations feel genuine to their audience.

Additionally, compliance with industry regulations is crucial. AI tools can monitor influencer content for compliance with advertising standards and guidelines, reducing the risk of non-compliance and associated penalties. This ensures that campaigns adhere to legal requirements and maintain transparency with audiences.

Conversely, AI can also help in identifying potential 'fake influencers'—those who artificially inflate their follower counts or engagement rates. By scrutinizing engagement patterns and follower authenticity, AI can help brands avoid fraudulent collaborations, further enhancing the efficacy of influencer marketing strategies.

Future Trends: The Evolution of AI in Influencer Marketing

As AI technology continues to evolve, its application in influencer marketing will only become more sophisticated. We can expect greater integration of machine learning, predictive analytics, and advanced data visualization, providing even richer insights and more targeted strategies.

For instance, AI could enable highly personalized influencer campaigns, where content is tailored not just to broad audience demographics but to individual preferences and behaviors. This level of personalization can drive deeper engagement and more meaningful connections between brands and consumers.

Advanced Sentiment Analysis: Improved sentiment analysis tools will provide insights into the emotional impact of influencer campaigns, helping brands understand how their collaborations resonate on an emotional level.

Enhanced Behavioral Predictions: AI's predictive capabilities will allow brands to anticipate consumer behavior and respond proactively, optimizing influencer marketing strategies in real time.

Virtual Influencers: AI-generated virtual influencers are an emerging trend. These digital avatars, controlled by AI, can engage audiences and promote products in ways that are uniquely engaging and innovative.

The possibilities are vast, and the potential for AI to redefine influencer marketing is immense. By embracing these technologies, brands can stay ahead of the curve and create influencer campaigns that are not only effective but also innovative and aligned with the ever-changing digital landscape.

In conclusion, AI is set to revolutionize influencer marketing. From identifying the perfect partners to managing relationships and measuring impact, AI streamlines the entire process and drives superior results. For marketing professionals and enthusiasts, leveraging AI in influencer marketing isn't just an option—it's a necessity for staying competitive and succeeding in today's digital age.

CHAPTER 13:
ENHANCING CUSTOMER LOYALTY PROGRAMS

Customer loyalty programs have been a staple in marketing strategies for decades. These programs aim to create a sense of belonging among customers and incentivize repeated business. However, the advent of artificial intelligence (AI) provides an expansive canvas for marketers to reimagine and enhance these loyalty programs, making them smarter, more personalized, and highly effective.

AI's capability to analyze vast amounts of data quickly and accurately is a game-changer. Gone are the days when loyalty programs were limited to simple point systems or tiered rewards. Today, AI can create multi-faceted, engaging, and dynamic loyalty ecosystems. By leveraging data-driven insights and predictive analytics, companies can tailor loyalty programs to individual customer preferences, behaviors, and purchasing patterns. This shift not only enhances customer satisfaction but also drives long-term business growth.

At the heart of AI-enhanced loyalty programs is personalization. Imagine a scenario where every touchpoint with the customer feels unique and personalized. AI systems can sift through massive datasets to identify individual preferences and tailor loyalty rewards accordingly. For instance, a customer who frequently purchases coffee might receive a personalized discount on their favorite brew, while a book lover might get early access to new releases or special book club events.

This level of personalization makes customers feel valued and understood, significantly boosting brand loyalty.

Leveraging Predictive Analytics

Predictive analytics plays a crucial role in enhancing customer loyalty programs. By analyzing historical data and identifying trends, AI can forecast future customer behavior. This predictive capability allows marketers to proactively engage with customers at critical moments. For example, if a customer's buying cycle indicates they are due for a repeat purchase, the system can automatically generate and deliver a personalized offer to prompt that purchase, effectively driving repeat business.

This foresight extends to identifying at-risk customers as well. AI can analyze engagement levels, frequency of purchases, and other behavioral metrics to flag individuals who are likely to disengage. Targeted interventions, such as personalized offers or re-engagement campaigns, can then be deployed to win back these customers. Predictive analytics thus shifts the loyalty program from a reactive to a proactive strategy, ensuring sustained customer engagement and retention.

Enhancing Customer Experience

The customer experience is pivotal in any loyalty program's success. AI-powered chatbots and virtual assistants can provide instant support and engagement, making customers feel valued and attended to. These bots can answer queries, provide personalized recommendations, and even assist in redeeming rewards, all in real-time. The immediacy and accuracy of AI responses enhance the overall customer experience, making interactions smooth and satisfying.

Moreover, AI can streamline the process of earning and redeeming rewards. Traditional loyalty programs often frustrate customers with complex rules and delayed gratifications. AI can simplify this by providing real-time updates on point balances, offering instant rewards, and ensuring seamless redemption processes. This efficiency not only boosts customer satisfaction but also encourages continued participation in the program.

Segmenting and Targeting

Customer segmentation is another area where AI shines. AI algorithms can analyze customer data to segment them into various groups based on purchasing behavior, preferences, and past interactions. These segments can then be targeted with tailored loyalty rewards and marketing campaigns. For example, high-value customers might receive exclusive offers, early access to new products, or VIP treatment, while occasional buyers might be incentivized with special discounts or loyalty points to encourage more frequent purchases.

This intelligent segmentation ensures that the right message reaches the right customer at the right time. By tailoring the loyalty experience to individual preferences and behaviors, brands can foster deeper connections and stronger loyalty among their customer base.

Integration with Other Marketing Strategies

Integrating AI-enhanced loyalty programs with other marketing strategies further amplifies their impact. For instance, combining loyalty programs with social media campaigns can drive higher engagement. AI can identify customers who are active on specific social platforms and create personalized social media offers or exclusive content. Encouraging customers to share their experiences or rewards online can increase brand visibility and attract new customers.

Additionally, AI can align loyalty programs with email marketing efforts. Personalized emails with tailored offers, reward updates, and special promotions can keep customers engaged and informed. The synergy between email marketing and loyalty programs can drive higher open rates, click-through rates, and ultimately, conversions.

The same is true for integrating loyalty programs with in-store experiences. AI can analyze in-store behavior through sensors and IoT devices to create personalized shopping experiences. For example, a customer entering the store can receive personalized greetings and recommendations based on their purchase history. This seamless blend of offline and online experiences can significantly enhance customer satisfaction and loyalty.

Measuring Success and Optimization

To ensure that AI-enhanced loyalty programs deliver the desired results, continuous measurement and optimization are essential. Key performance indicators (KPIs) such as customer retention rates, repeat purchase rates, average spend per customer, and overall program engagement should be monitored regularly. AI can assist in this by providing detailed analytics and insights into program performance.

Furthermore, AI-driven A/B testing can optimize loyalty program elements. By testing different offers, reward structures, and communication strategies, marketers can identify what resonates best with their audience and refine their approach accordingly. This iterative process ensures that the loyalty program evolves with changing customer preferences and market dynamics, maintaining its effectiveness and relevance.

In summary, AI has the potential to revolutionize customer loyalty programs. By harnessing the power of data-driven insights, predictive analytics, and personalization, marketers can create loyalty programs that are not only engaging but also highly effective. The result is a win-win for both customers and brands—customers receive personalized experiences and rewards that make them feel valued, and brands benefit from increased customer retention, higher lifetime value, and sustained business growth.

As we continue to explore and embrace the opportunities AI presents, it is crucial to remember that the ultimate goal is to enhance the human experience. AI is a powerful tool, but it should be used to complement, not replace, the empathy and understanding that lie at the heart of all successful customer relationships. By striking the right balance, we can create loyalty programs that truly resonate with customers and drive lasting success.

CHAPTER 14:
SENTIMENT ANALYSIS

In the buzzing world of marketing, understanding how your audience feels about your brand is priceless. This is where sentiment analysis steps in. It's like having a superpower that allows you to gauge public sentiment on social media, reviews, forums, and more, without breaking a sweat. Essentially, sentiment analysis employs artificial intelligence to determine the overall attitude, whether positive, negative, or neutral, expressed in a piece of text.

Why does it matter so much? Because in today's digital landscape, every tweet, post, and review can influence a potential customer's perception. For marketing professionals, being able to measure sentiment means you can react swiftly, tailor your strategy in real time, and ultimately, foster stronger relationships with your audience. Imagine catching a wave of dissatisfaction before it becomes a tsunami or riding the crest of positive feedback to amplify your brand's success.

At its core, sentiment analysis involves natural language processing (NLP), machine learning, and sometimes deep learning. These technologies work together to dissect, evaluate, and assign sentiment scores to various pieces of text. The process usually begins with text preprocessing, which includes steps like tokenization, stemming, and removing stop words. This cleanup makes the text easier for algorithms to analyze.

Once the text is preprocessed, machine learning models—trained on vast datasets—come into play. These models can recognize sentiment-bearing words and phrases and weigh them according to context. For example, "unpredictable" could be negative for a product review but positive for a thriller novel. The sophistication of these models means they can understand nuances in language, including sarcasm, slang, and emoticons, which were challenging for traditional algorithms.

But sentiment analysis isn't just for social media monitoring. It has a myriad of applications across different facets of marketing. Take customer service as an example. By integrating sentiment analysis into chatbots, companies can identify and prioritize queries that require urgent attention, thereby improving response times and customer satisfaction. In product development, sentiment analysis helps in gathering insights from customer feedback, guiding you to improve or innovate based on real opinions and needs.

When implementing sentiment analysis, there are some important metrics to consider. Precision and recall, for example, are vital in evaluating the performance of sentiment analysis models. Precision measures the accuracy of positive predictions, while recall evaluates the model's ability to capture all relevant instances. Balancing these metrics often involves tuning your algorithms and continuously feeding them more data to learn from.

It's also crucial to understand that sentiment analysis isn't foolproof. Misinterpretations can happen due to language complexity, ambiguous phrasing, or cultural differences. For instance, the phrase "wickedly good" would pose a challenge. Such issues underline the importance of continually refining algorithms and perhaps even employing human-in-the-loop approaches to ensure the highest accuracy.

Another compelling use case for sentiment analysis in marketing is competitive benchmarking. By analyzing sentiment around your competitors' brands, you can glean insights into their strengths and weaknesses from a consumer perspective. This can guide your own marketing strategies, helping you to capitalize on their shortcomings and learn from their successes.

Moreover, sentiment analysis can be instrumental in influencer marketing. It's not just about choosing influencers with the highest follower counts anymore. By analyzing the sentiment of their audience's reactions, you can select influencers whose followers genuinely appreciate and resonate with their content, ensuring a more authentic and productive partnership.

In the sphere of content marketing, sentiment analysis can help you fine-tune your messaging. By analyzing how different sections of your audience react to various types of content, you can tailor your future posts to evoke the desired sentiment. Whether you're aiming to inspire, entertain, or inform, sentiment analysis provides the data-driven insights needed to craft impactful content.

It's worth noting that the tools and platforms available for sentiment analysis are continually evolving. Established platforms like IBM Watson, Google Cloud's Natural Language, and Microsoft Text Analytics offer robust sentiment analysis capabilities that are easy to integrate into your marketing stack. These tools often come with user-friendly dashboards that visualize sentiment trends, making it simpler to monitor and act on insights.

As powerful as sentiment analysis is, it should never be viewed in isolation. Context is critical. For instance, a sudden spike in negative sentiment could be due to a temporary glitch or external factors unrelated to your brand's performance. Combining sentiment analysis with other data points like customer behavior metrics and sales data can provide a more holistic view and help in making more informed decisions.

Furthermore, as privacy becomes an increasingly prominent concern, it's crucial to ensure that your methods of gathering data for sentiment analysis comply with relevant regulations. Transparency about data usage will not only keep you compliant but also build trust with your audience, who will appreciate your commitment to their privacy.

To wrap it up, sentiment analysis offers a treasure trove of insights for marketers willing to tap into its potential. It empowers you to understand and respond to the emotional pulse of your audience, thereby crafting more effective and engaging marketing strategies. While it isn't without its challenges, the benefits far outweigh the complexities when executed correctly. In the evolving landscape of AI-driven marketing, mastering sentiment analysis is not just an option—it's a necessity.

As we prepare to dive deeper into the analytics realm, remember that sentiment analysis is an ongoing process. Continuous learning and adaptation will keep you ahead of the curve, ensuring your brand not only meets but exceeds customer expectations.

Conclusion

In a marketplace brimming with choices, understanding how your audience feels can set you apart. Sentiment analysis, with its deep dive into consumer emotions, equips you with the knowledge to make smarter, more empathetic decisions. This chapter laid the groundwork; the next chapters will build on it, revealing even more sophisticated uses of AI in marketing. Stay tuned as we explore tools, ethics, and real-world applications that will transform the way you engage with your audience and help you achieve phenomenal results.

CHAPTER 15:
AI FOR MARKET RESEARCH

Market research has always been a cornerstone of effective marketing strategies. Understanding your target audience, their preferences, and behaviors can make the difference between a campaign that resonates and one that falls flat. With the surge of artificial intelligence (AI), market research is undergoing a paradigm shift, bringing unprecedented levels of accuracy, efficiency, and depth to the process.

AI for market research leverages advanced algorithms and machine learning techniques to analyze vast amounts of data and extract meaningful insights. Gone are the days when marketers relied solely on surveys and focus groups to gather information. Today, AI tools can sift through social media posts, online reviews, transaction data, and more to unveil a comprehensive understanding of consumer sentiment and trends.

One of the most significant advantages of using AI in market research is its ability to process large volumes of data quickly. Traditional market research methods can be time-consuming and labor-intensive, but AI can analyze data in real-time, providing actionable insights almost instantaneously. This speed allows marketers to be more agile and responsive to changing market conditions.

Furthermore, AI-driven market research tools can identify patterns and correlations that might be missed by human analysts. These tools use natural language processing (NLP) and predictive analytics to interpret textual data, understanding the nuances of consumer sentiment and predicting future trends. This capability enables marketers to stay ahead of the curve and make informed decisions that drive business growth.

Another critical aspect of AI in market research is its capacity for personalization. By analyzing individual customer data, AI can segment audiences into highly specific groups based on their behaviors, preferences, and interactions. This granular level of understanding allows marketers to tailor their messages and offers to different segments, enhancing the relevance and effectiveness of their campaigns.

Consider the example of a company launching a new product. Traditional market research methods might involve conducting surveys and focus groups to gauge interest and gather feedback. While these methods are valuable, they can be limited in scope and scale. AI tools, on the other hand, can analyze social media conversations, search engine data, and purchase histories to provide a more comprehensive understanding of consumer attitudes and behaviors towards the product.

Moreover, AI can enhance market research by providing predictive analytics. Predictive models use historical data and machine learning algorithms to forecast future trends and consumer behaviors. This foresight allows marketers to anticipate market demands and adjust their strategies accordingly, reducing the risk of costly missteps.

The integration of AI into market research also opens up new possibilities for sentiment analysis. By analyzing social media posts, online reviews, and customer feedback, AI tools can gauge the overall sentiment towards a brand or product. This sentiment analysis provides valuable insights into how consumers feel and think, allowing marketers to address concerns and capitalize on positive perceptions.

Additionally, AI can help identify and track emerging trends. By continuously monitoring various data sources, AI tools can detect shifts in consumer preferences and behaviors, enabling marketers to seize opportunities and stay ahead of competitors. This trend analysis is particularly valuable in fast-paced industries where staying relevant is crucial.

Despite its numerous advantages, the use of AI in market research is not without challenges. One of the primary concerns is the quality and accuracy of the data being analyzed. AI models are only as good as the data they are trained on, and poor-quality data can lead to erroneous conclusions. Therefore, it's essential to ensure that data is clean, accurate, and representative of the target audience.

Another challenge is the potential for bias in AI algorithms. If the data used to train the AI models is biased, the resulting insights will also be biased. Marketers must be vigilant in identifying and mitigating any biases to ensure that their decisions are based on objective and accurate information.

Moreover, there are ethical considerations to take into account. The use of AI in market research often involves collecting and analyzing large amounts of personal data. Marketers must ensure that they comply with data privacy regulations and maintain the trust of their customers by handling their data responsibly and transparently.

To effectively harness the power of AI for market research, marketing professionals need to choose the right tools and platforms. There are numerous AI-driven market research solutions available, ranging from social listening tools to customer feedback analysis platforms. Selecting the right tool depends on the specific needs and goals of the business.

It's also crucial to invest in the necessary skills and expertise. While AI tools can automate many aspects of market research, human oversight and interpretation are still essential. Marketers need to understand how to use these tools effectively and interpret the insights they generate to make informed decisions.

Training and upskilling the marketing team in AI and data analytics can provide significant advantages. Familiarity with AI concepts and techniques will enable marketers to leverage the full potential of AI-driven market research and stay ahead in an increasingly competitive landscape.

In conclusion, AI is revolutionizing market research by providing deeper, more accurate, and timely insights into consumer behavior and trends. By leveraging AI tools for data analysis, sentiment detection, and predictive modeling, marketing professionals can make more informed decisions, enhance their strategies, and ultimately achieve better results. Embracing AI in market research is not just a trend; it's a strategic imperative for any business looking to thrive in the digital age.

As we continue to explore the impact of AI on different aspects of marketing, it's essential to stay focused on the goal: improving customer engagement and achieving measurable results. The journey of integrating AI into market research is just one piece of the puzzle, but it's a critical one that can provide a solid foundation for all other marketing activities.

CHAPTER 16:
ETHICS AND PRIVACY IN AI MARKETING

Marketing professionals are well aware that artificial intelligence (AI) has revolutionized our industry, offering unprecedented capabilities to reach and engage customers. However, with great power comes great responsibility. The ethical considerations and privacy concerns associated with AI in marketing are paramount. Navigating these issues isn't just about compliance; it's about building trust and fostering long-term customer relationships.

One of the most pressing ethical questions revolves around data usage. AI-driven marketing relies heavily on data to make predictions, personalize experiences, and automate tasks. But where does this data come from? More importantly, do customers know how their data is being used? Transparency in data collection and usage is essential. Marketers need to inform customers about what data is being collected, how it will be used, and ensure they have the option to opt-out if they choose.

Beyond transparency, the concept of consent is crucial. Merely informing customers isn't enough; explicit consent must be obtained. This goes hand-in-hand with regulations such as the General Data Protection Regulation (GDPR) in the European Union and the California Consumer Privacy Act (CCPA) in the United States. These regulations mandate stringent consumer data protection measures, affirming the need for marketers to respect and protect individual privacy.

Another significant ethical aspect is bias in AI algorithms. AI models are only as good as the data they are trained on. If the data is biased, the results will be too. For example, if an AI tool is used to segment customers for targeted advertising and the underlying data is biased, certain groups may either be unfairly targeted or neglected. Addressing this issue requires a conscious effort to ensure diversity and representation in training data, along with regular audits of AI systems to detect and mitigate bias.

Privacy and security concerns also extend to how data is stored and protected. Data breaches can have devastating effects not only on customers but also on the trust and reputation of the organization involved. Marketers must collaborate closely with IT and cybersecurity teams to implement robust security measures. Encryption, anonymization, and secure data storage practices are critical components of a sound data protection strategy.

In addition to protecting customer data, marketers should consider the ethical implications of AI decision-making processes. One area that has garnered attention is the use of AI for personalization. While personalized marketing can greatly enhance customer experience, there is a thin line between helpful customization and intrusive behavior. Marketers must strike a balance, ensuring that personalization initiatives are genuinely beneficial and not perceived as invasive.

Moreover, AI ethics in marketing isn't confined to data and privacy; it extends to how AI technology impacts employment. Automation, for instance, has the potential to displace jobs. While AI can significantly boost efficiency and outcomes, it's essential to weigh the benefits against the socio-economic implications. Organizations should look at AI as an augmentation tool rather than a replacement, using it to complement human efforts. This can involve reskilling and upskilling employees to work alongside AI, leveraging both human creativity and AI's analytical prowess.

One approach to tackle these ethical issues is the formation of cross-functional ethics committees within organizations. Such committees should include members from diverse disciplines—marketing, legal, IT, and human resources—to holistically assess the ethical implications of AI projects. Regular reviews and updates of AI ethics policies keep the organization aligned with evolving standards and societal expectations.

The adoption of AI ethics frameworks is another powerful tool. Frameworks provide structured guidelines to ensure AI systems are designed and deployed responsibly. Many organizations and institutions have developed such frameworks, offering resources that can be adapted to fit specific business needs. Key principles often include fairness, accountability, transparency, and user empowerment, forming a solid foundation for ethical AI practices.

Another vital aspect is educating and training the marketing team about ethical AI use. Marketing professionals need to be well-versed in ethical considerations and privacy laws, ensuring that these principles are deeply embedded in the organization's culture. Continuous learning opportunities, workshops, and certifications can help keep the team informed and vigilant.

To truly embed ethics and privacy into AI marketing, organizations must adopt a customer-centric approach. Respecting customer preferences and valuing their trust should be at the core of all marketing activities. For instance, obtaining feedback on satisfaction with how their data is used and addressing any concerns they might have can foster a culture of trust and transparency. In the end, when customers feel valued and respected, they are likely to stay loyal and advocate for the brand.

In conclusion, integrating ethics and privacy into AI marketing isn't simply a regulatory requirement—it's a crucial component of building trustworthy and sustainable customer relationships. As AI continues to transform the marketing landscape, the need for ethical vigilance and a strong commitment to privacy will only grow. By proactively addressing these challenges, marketers can leverage AI's immense potential while safeguarding the foundational elements of trust and respect. Adopting an ethical framework, ensuring data transparency, and prioritizing customer consent are just the beginning. It's about continuously striving to create a balanced, equitable, and secure marketing ecosystem.

Chapter 17:
Tools and Platforms for AI Marketing

In the transformative landscape of AI marketing, tools and platforms serve as the essential enablers. These instruments are not just extras; they are foundational to successfully integrating AI into your marketing strategies. With the right tools, you can elevate customer engagement, streamline your marketing processes, and yield measurable results.

First, let's delve into customer relationship management (CRM) systems with integrated AI capabilities. Platforms like Salesforce and HubSpot have revolutionized how marketers interact with and understand their customers. AI enhances these CRMs by predicting customer behavior, personalizing user experiences, and providing actionable insights. Imagine sending an email that not only addresses a customer's needs at the exact moment they have it but also predicts future needs. This type of precision is where AI-powered CRMs excel.

Next, we have marketing automation platforms. These platforms, such as Marketo and ActiveCampaign, leverage AI to automate repetitive tasks and refine marketing campaigns. Automation isn't just about sending an email; it's about orchestrating multi-channel campaigns that adapt in real-time based on user interactions. By analyzing vast datasets, AI can identify patterns and trends that humans might miss, optimizing messaging and timing to improve engagement rates comprehensively.

Social media management tools have also significantly benefited from AI integrations. Hootsuite and Sprout Social, for instance, use AI to predict the best times to post, understand trending topics, and even automate responses. These AI-driven insights mean your social media strategy can become more responsive and proactive, rather than reactive.

Voice and conversational AI tools, including chatbots, are indispensable in modern marketing. Platforms like Drift and Intercom provide ways to create conversational interfaces that can engage customers 24/7. These aren't just basic question-answer systems; advanced chatbots can handle complex tasks like booking appointments, processing orders, or even providing personalized recommendations based on user data. Conversational AI can dramatically improve customer service while freeing human agents to handle more nuanced issues.

Let's not overlook content creation tools. Platforms like Jasper and Phrasee utilize AI to generate copy that aligns with your brand voice, SEO strategies, and target audience preferences. Whether it's blog posts, email subject lines, or social media updates, AI-driven content tools can save you time and ensure your messaging remains consistent and effective. These tools analyze current trends and audience engagement metrics to offer suggestions that resonate with your audience.

AI is also making strides in the realm of predictive analytics. Tools like Google Analytics and IBM Watson can analyze past consumer behavior to predict future actions. This predictive capacity allows marketers to be proactive rather than reactive. For example, you can anticipate a customer's next purchase or identify when they are likely to churn, enabling you to take preemptive measures to retain them.

Advertising platforms such as Google Ads and Facebook Ads Manager have incorporated AI to optimize ad spend and targeting. These tools no longer require marketers to manually select demographics or guess where their ad dollars will be best spent. AI algorithms can analyze a wealth of data points to place ads in front of the most receptive users, enhancing ROI and minimizing wasted spend.

E-commerce benefits immensely from AI tools like Shopify's Kit and Adobe's Sensei. These platforms can personalize the shopping experience by recommending products based on user behavior and preferences. They can also optimize pricing dynamically by assessing market trends and competitor pricing in real-time. This level of personalization can significantly boost conversion rates and average order values.

In terms of analytics and reporting, tools like Tableau and Looker provide AI-driven insights that surpass traditional data analysis methods. These platforms can visualize complex data sets in ways that are easy to understand and act upon. They enable you to make informed decisions quickly, based on real-time data and predictive analytics.

Furthermore, sentiment analysis tools like MonkeyLearn and Lexalytics allow marketers to tap into public sentiment around their brands. These tools analyze social media, customer reviews, and other forms of user-generated content to provide insights into how your brand is perceived. Understanding the sentiment behind the data helps you respond more effectively to customer needs and improve your overall brand strategy.

Email marketing is another domain where AI has made significant inroads. Platforms like Mailchimp and SendinBlue use AI to optimize email campaigns by analyzing what types of content generate the highest engagement. They can also personalize email frequency and timing based on individual user behavior, ensuring that your messages reach users at the optimal times.

In the video marketing space, platforms like Vidyard and Wistia use AI to analyze viewer engagement and suggest improvements. These tools can identify which parts of your video content are most engaging and why, allowing you to refine your video marketing strategy continually. AI can also personalize video content at scale, ensuring that each viewer sees the most relevant material based on their preferences and behavior.

Voice search optimization tools like Google's Voice Search and Microsoft's Cortana Analytics are becoming increasingly important. With the rise of smart speakers and voice-activated assistants, optimizing for voice search has become crucial. These tools help marketers understand the natural language queries that users are likely to employ, enabling the creation of content that ranks well in voice search results.

AI-powered recommendation systems are indispensable for content-driven platforms. Whether it's Netflix suggesting a new show or Amazon recommending a product, these recommendation engines analyze user behavior in real-time to provide relevant suggestions. Implementing similar systems on your platforms can enhance user engagement and retention.

Finally, let's touch on the ethical and operational considerations of deploying AI tools. While the advantages are compelling, it's vital to ensure that these tools are used responsibly. This means being transparent with your customers about how their data is used and ensuring compliance with regulations like GDPR and CCPA. Ethical AI usage builds trust and can enhance your brand's reputation.

To summarize, the array of AI tools and platforms available today can revolutionize the way you approach marketing. By integrating these technologies, you're not just keeping up with the competition; you're setting a new standard for what's possible. From CRM systems and marketing automation platforms to content creation and sentiment analysis tools, each plays a pivotal role in creating a cohesive, effective, and forward-thinking marketing strategy. As you explore these tools, remember that the ultimate goal is to enhance customer engagement, optimize your efforts, and drive measurable results. In the constantly evolving landscape of AI marketing, being equipped with the right tools isn't just beneficial; it's essential.

CHAPTER 18:
IMPLEMENTING AI IN SMALL BUSINESSES

Small businesses often find themselves at a crossroads when it comes to leveraging advanced technologies like artificial intelligence (AI). The common misconception is that AI is only for the big players—those with hefty budgets and dedicated tech teams. Yet, this simply isn't the case. Small businesses can, and should, embrace AI to improve their marketing efficacy, operational efficiency, and customer engagement. Here's how they can do just that.

First, it's vital to start small. AI can indeed seem intimidating, but you don't need to overhaul your entire operation overnight. Begin by identifying specific areas where AI can make an immediate impact. Think about your daily business tasks that consume the most time or those requiring rigorous decision-making processes. Email marketing automation, for instance, can drastically reduce the hours spent on campaign management and improve the targeting of email blasts.

This leads us to the importance of choosing the right tools and platforms. There are numerous AI solutions tailored for small businesses, many of which are cost-effective and user-friendly. Tools like HubSpot, Mailchimp, and Buffer offer AI-powered features that can help you automate emails, schedule social media posts, and even analyze customer behavior. Selecting such tools can provide an entry point into the world of AI without the need for large financial investments.

Another critical aspect to consider is data collection. Small businesses often overlook the power of data they already have. Customer emails, purchase histories, and website engagement metrics are gold mines for AI-driven analytics. By integrating AI with existing CRM systems, small businesses can gain insights into customer behavior, allowing for more targeted marketing and personalized customer experiences.

Speaking of personalization, AI excels in creating bespoke customer experiences by predicting needs and preferences. For example, AI can analyze browsing patterns to offer personalized product recommendations. This doesn't just improve customer satisfaction but can also boost sales. Tools like Amazon Personalize are available for small businesses to implement high-level personalization strategies with relative ease.

AI can also greatly enhance customer service, an area that small businesses often struggle to compete in due to limited resources. Utilizing chatbots can reduce the strain on customer service teams by handling routine inquiries. These chatbots can be trained using natural language processing (NLP) to offer solutions, book appointments, or even process orders efficiently. More sophisticated bots can escalate complex issues to human agents, ensuring customers always feel supported.

For small businesses dependent on local foot traffic or direct sales, AI can offer predictive analytics to streamline inventory and supply chain management. AI tools can forecast demand based on historic sales data, current trends, and even seasonal variations. By optimizing stock levels, businesses can reduce wastage and prevent stockouts, thus maintaining a smooth flow of operations.

Financial constraints often act as a barrier to adopting new technologies, but there are affordable AI solutions designed specifically for small businesses. Google Analytics, for instance, offers AI-driven insights into website traffic and user behavior, allowing businesses to optimize their online presence without a heavy price tag. Another example is Grammarly, an AI-powered tool for improving written communication, a critical aspect of marketing that small businesses can't afford to overlook.

Implementation isn't just about choosing tools and collecting data; it's also about fostering an AI-ready culture within the organization. Training and development are crucial. Employees must understand not just how to use the tools but also the broader implications of AI on business strategy and customer experience. Webinars, workshops, and online courses can be effective ways to upskill your team in AI literacy.

A significant hurdle that small businesses might face is the integration of AI with existing systems. It's essential to conduct a thorough analysis of your current technology landscape. Ensure the chosen AI tools are compatible with your existing software and processes. Open-source platforms like TensorFlow can be invaluable, providing the flexibility to develop custom AI models that can be integrated into the existing framework.

On the subject of custom AI models, small businesses should not shy away from exploring this option. While off-the-shelf solutions are convenient and effective, having bespoke models tailored to specific business needs can offer a competitive edge. For instance, a local retail store could develop a model that forecasts sales based on local events, weather conditions, and even social media sentiment analysis. Collaborating with freelance data scientists or academic institutions can make this more feasible and affordable.

Once implemented, it's crucial to continuously monitor and refine AI applications. AI is not a set-it-and-forget-it solution. Regularly reviewing performance metrics, collecting feedback, and making adjustments ensures that AI tools evolve in tandem with your business needs.

An iterative approach helps in maximizing the ROI from your AI investments and keeps your business agile.

Moreover, small businesses should utilize the community and networks available to them. Participating in forums, attending industry conferences, and joining local business groups can provide valuable insights and peer support. These platforms often share success stories and case studies that offer practical guidance on AI implementation. Learning from others' experiences can help avoid common pitfalls and accelerate your AI journey.

Security and ethical considerations also play a pivotal role. Small businesses might be more vulnerable to data breaches, making it essential to ensure that AI tools comply with data protection regulations such as GDPR. Maintaining transparency with customers about how their data is used builds trust and fortifies your brand's reputation.

In summary, implementing AI in small businesses is not just feasible but highly beneficial. Starting small, choosing the right tools, leveraging existing data, and fostering an AI-ready culture can set the stage for successful AI adoption. Continuous monitoring, community engagement, and ethical practices will ensure that AI becomes a core component of your business strategy. By taking these steps, small businesses can harness the transformative power of AI to compete more effectively and achieve sustainable growth.

CHAPTER 19:
CASE STUDIES OF AI IN MARKETING

Examining the influence of artificial intelligence across various marketing sectors offers a vivid testament to its transformative power. From gigantic retailers leveraging AI to tailor customer experiences and skyrocket sales, to financial institutions utilizing AI for hyper-personalized financial advice, the implications are vast and inspiring. Each case study encapsulates innovative approaches and tangible results, highlighting real-world applications that resonate profoundly with the goals of modern marketers. By dissecting these examples, marketing professionals can glean actionable insights and strategies that clearly showcase how AI technology can revolutionize their own efforts, driving both efficiency and success.

Chapter 19.1: Retail Industry

The retail industry stands as one of the most transformative sectors when it comes to embracing artificial intelligence in marketing. From the surge of personalized recommendations on your favorite e-commerce site to tailored promotional emails, AI is revolutionizing how retailers engage with their customers. This section delves into real-world case studies showcasing the powerful impact of AI on retail marketing strategies.

One of the most compelling examples is Amazon. Leveraging machine learning algorithms, Amazon has perfected the art of recommendation engines. When a customer logs into Amazon, they are greeted with products specifically chosen based on past behavior, search history, and even purchase patterns of users with similar profiles. This targeted approach has significantly increased click-through rates and conversions, contributing to Amazon's profound success.

Similarly, Sephora, a leading beauty retailer, has taken customer engagement to another level with its AI-powered tools. By using chatbots and virtual assistants, Sephora allows customers to get personalized beauty advice and product recommendations without ever setting foot in a store. These chatbots use natural language processing to understand customer inquiries and provide tailored responses, which not only enhance the customer experience but also streamline the shopping process.

Walmart is another retail giant making waves with AI. The company uses predictive analytics to manage inventory effectively, ensuring that shelves are stocked with the right products at the right time. By analyzing customer data, weather forecasts, and even social media trends, Walmart can predict which products will be in high demand, thus reducing waste and increasing sales. Furthermore, their use of AI in pricing strategy allows for dynamic pricing that reacts to market changes in real-time, optimizing revenue.

Let's not overlook the behind-the-scenes magic of AI in retail logistics. Stores like Zara have integrated AI to streamline their supply chains. They use machine learning algorithms to predict fashion trends, which informs their design and production processes. This allows Zara to quickly turn around new styles, keeping their inventory fresh and highly relevant to consumer preferences.

Beyond these giants, smaller retailers are tapping into AI-driven personalization techniques. For example, Stitch Fix, an online personal styling service, uses a blend of human expertise and AI algorithms to deliver personalized clothing recommendations to their customers. By collecting data on customer preferences and feedback, Stich Fix continually refines its recommendations, making each shopping experience unique and highly tailored.

Another noteworthy example is The North Face, which employs IBM's Watson to provide intelligent shopping assistants. By asking customers a series of questions about their needs and preferences, Watson can recommend products that are best suited to individual customer requirements. This AI-driven service has significantly improved customer satisfaction and engagement.

The potential of AI in retail marketing extends to enhancing customer loyalty programs as well. Starbucks, for instance, uses AI to deliver personalized rewards and promotions through its mobile app. By analyzing purchase history and customer preferences, Starbucks can create tailored offers that encourage repeat business, thereby boosting customer loyalty and lifetime value.

Even physical stores are not left behind in this AI revolution. Lowe's, the home improvement retailer, introduced LoweBot, an in-store robot assistant. The robot assists customers in navigating the store, locating products, and providing product information. LoweBot uses AI to understand customer queries and guide them effectively, enriching the in-store shopping experience.

AI in retail marketing is also about creating seamless omnichannel experiences. Retailers like Macy's and Nordstrom have integrated AI across their online and physical channels to deliver a consistent and personalized shopping experience. By analyzing customer data collected from various touchpoints, these retailers can tailor marketing messages and product recommendations, whether the customer is shopping online or in-store.

One transformative aspect of AI in retail marketing is the ability to harness data for hyper-personalized experiences. AI enables retailers to analyze vast amounts of customer data to uncover hidden patterns and insights. For instance, by utilizing AI-driven sentiment analysis, retailers can understand customer emotions and perceptions, allowing them to tailor marketing strategies that resonate on a deeper emotional level.

Moreover, AI's role in visual search technology is revolutionizing the online shopping experience. Retailers like ASOS and H&M are leveraging AI-powered visual search tools that allow customers to upload images of fashion items they like and receive similar product recommendations from the retailer's catalog. This innovation streamlines the shopping process and enhances customer satisfaction by helping them find exactly what they are looking for.

Another exciting development is the use of augmented reality (AR) powered by AI in retail. IKEA, for instance, offers an AR app that allows customers to visualize how furniture would look in their homes before making a purchase. This AI-driven tool not only enhances the shopping experience but also reduces the likelihood of returns, as customers have a clearer expectation of the product.

Personalized email marketing is another area where AI is making a significant impact. Retailers like Uniqlo and Best Buy use AI to craft personalized email campaigns tailored to individual customer preferences and behavior. By analyzing data such as purchase history, browsing behavior, and past interactions, these retailers can send personalized offers and product recommendations that are more likely to convert.

In essence, the application of AI in retail marketing is about enhancing the customer journey at every touchpoint. Whether through personalized recommendations, intelligent chatbots, predictive analytics, or AR experiences, AI empowers retailers to engage with customers in more meaningful and effective ways. The ultimate goal is to create a seamless, personalized, and delightful shopping experience that drives customer loyalty and business growth.

One thing is certain: the fusion of AI and retail marketing is setting new standards for customer engagement and operational efficiency. As AI technology continues to evolve, its applications in retail will only become more sophisticated and impactful, offering endless opportunities for marketers to innovate and excel.

The retail industry's adoption of AI is not merely a trend but a fundamental shift in how businesses operate and interact with customers. It's a demonstration of how powerful AI can be in driving business success through enhanced marketing strategies. Going forward, the challenge for retail marketers will be to stay ahead of the curve by continuously exploring new AI technologies and applications that can further elevate the customer experience and achieve measurable results.

Chapter 19.2: Financial Services

Financial services have witnessed remarkable transformations with the integration of artificial intelligence (AI) into marketing strategies. Among the earliest adopters of AI, financial institutions leverage sophisticated algorithms to enhance customer experiences, optimize marketing efforts, and ultimately drive growth. This chapter delves into the various ways AI is revolutionizing marketing within the financial sector, presenting real-world case studies and actionable insights.

One of the most compelling examples of AI in financial services marketing is its role in customer segmentation and targeting. Financial institutions possess vast amounts of customer data, from transaction histories to behavioral insights, that can be harnessed through AI for precise targeting. By leveraging machine learning algorithms, banks can segment their customers into highly specific groups based on various parameters such as spending habits, life stages, and financial goals. This allows for the creation of highly personalized marketing campaigns that are much more likely to resonate with individual customers.

For instance, a leading multinational bank utilized AI-driven segmentation to identify customers likely to be interested in home loans. By analyzing transaction data and financial behaviors, the bank tailored its marketing efforts to this specific segment, providing personalized loan offers and targeted content. The result was a significant uptick in home loan conversions and customer engagement, illustrating the power of AI in refining targeting strategies.

Additionally, AI-driven chatbots have become a cornerstone of customer service in the financial sector. These intelligent virtual assistants handle a myriad of customer queries, from balance inquiries to fraudulent transaction reports, around the clock. By integrating chatbots into their marketing strategies, financial institutions can offer seamless and efficient service, enhancing customer satisfaction while reducing operational costs.

A noteworthy case study involves a regional credit union that implemented an AI chatbot to manage customer inquiries on its mobile banking app. The chatbot, equipped with natural language processing (NLP) capabilities, handled over 60% of customer interactions without human intervention. This not only streamlined operations but also allowed the credit union to allocate human resources to more complex tasks, thereby improving overall service quality.

Moreover, predictive analytics powered by AI is transforming how financial services forecast customer behaviors and market trends. By analyzing historical data and identifying patterns, AI algorithms can predict future customer actions, enabling proactive marketing approaches. Predictive models can forecast which customers are likely to churn, which products they might be interested in, and how their financial behaviors could evolve over time.

A case in point is an investment firm that employed predictive analytics to identify clients who might benefit from wealth management services. By analyzing data points such as income levels, investment history, and market trends, the firm crafted targeted campaigns offering personalized financial advice and services. This approach not only boosted client engagement but also increased the uptake of wealth management products, significantly contributing to the firm's revenue growth.

Personalization, an increasingly critical aspect of marketing in the digital age, is taken to new heights with AI in the financial sector. Financial institutions are utilizing AI to deliver highly personalized experiences to their customers. By analyzing individual customer data, AI systems can offer tailored product recommendations, personalized content, and custom financial advice, making each interaction relevant and valuable.

Consider the example of a digital bank that used AI to personalize its marketing communications. By integrating AI into its email marketing platform, the bank sent out tailored emails based on the recipient's transaction history, financial goals, and online behaviors. These personalized emails saw a 30% higher open rate and a 20% increase in conversion rate compared to generic marketing emails, underscoring the efficacy of AI-driven personalization.

Another area where AI is making strides in financial services marketing is through sentiment analysis. By analyzing social media conversations, customer reviews, and other forms of unstructured data, financial institutions can gauge public sentiment towards their brand, products, and services. This real-time insight allows for more responsive and adaptive marketing strategies that align with customer sentiments.

For example, a major insurance company used AI-powered sentiment analysis to monitor customer feedback on social media platforms. By identifying negative sentiments and trending issues, the company swiftly addressed concerns while crafting marketing messages that resonated with positive customer experiences. This real-time adaptability not only enhanced the company's brand perception but also bolstered customer loyalty.

AI's role in automating marketing campaigns cannot be overstated. Automation tools driven by AI enable financial institutions to run complex marketing campaigns with unprecedented efficiency. From email workflows to social media advertising, AI automates repetitive tasks, allowing marketing teams to focus on strategy and creativity. Automated campaigns also allow for real-time adjustments based on performance metrics, ensuring optimal outcomes.

A prime example can be found in a financial services firm that automated its cross-selling campaigns using AI. By integrating AI into their customer relationship management (CRM) system, the firm executed highly targeted email and SMS campaigns promoting complementary financial products. The automation not only saved time and resources but also resulted in a 25% increase in cross-sell conversions, demonstrating the significant impact of AI-driven automation.

In conclusion, the financial services sector is at the forefront of leveraging AI for marketing innovation. Whether through customer segmentation, chatbots, predictive analytics, personalization, sentiment analysis, or automation, AI is empowering financial institutions to execute smarter, more effective marketing strategies. These advancements not only enhance customer engagement and satisfaction but also drive tangible business outcomes, proving the transformative potential of AI in financial services marketing.

CHAPTER 20:
MEASURING ROI IN AI MARKETING

A s artificial intelligence continues to transform the marketing landscape, understanding how to measure return on investment (ROI) becomes crucial. ROI in AI marketing isn't just a vanity metric; it's a fundamental gauge of success that informs future decisions and justifies investments. The challenge, however, lies in accurately capturing the multifaceted benefits and costs associated with AI initiatives.

First, let's address why measuring ROI in AI marketing is different from traditional marketing efforts. AI, by its nature, introduces layers of complexity. It combines various data sources, employs intricate algorithms, and often interacts with other technological components in the marketing ecosystem. To capture ROI effectively, marketers should adopt a holistic approach that encompasses both tangible and intangible benefits.

One of the tangible benefits of AI in marketing is cost efficiency. AI-driven tools can automate repetitive tasks, reducing man-hours and operational costs significantly. For example, AI chatbots can handle customer queries 24/7, freeing up human agents for more complex tasks. Another tangible benefit is enhanced targeting precision. By analyzing vast datasets, AI can identify high-value customers more accurately, reducing waste in ad spend and increasing conversion rates.

But tangible benefits are just one side of the coin. AI also brings several intangible benefits that can be harder to quantify yet equally important. Improved customer experience is a prime example. AI personalization algorithms can deliver tailored content, making customers feel valued and understood. Over time, this fosters customer loyalty and boosts lifetime value.

To measure ROI effectively, marketers must start with clear objectives and key performance indicators (KPIs). This involves aligning AI initiatives with broader business goals. Are you looking to increase sales, improve customer satisfaction, or enhance operational efficiency? Each objective will have different KPIs. For instance, if your goal is to boost sales, key metrics might include conversion rates, average order value, and customer acquisition costs.

One effective strategy for measuring ROI is to conduct A/B testing. This involves comparing the performance of AI-driven campaigns with traditional ones. By evaluating metrics pre- and post-implementation, you can isolate the impact of AI. Additionally, A/B testing allows for a controlled environment in which variables are minimized, providing a clearer picture of AI's effectiveness.

Another technique is the use of attribution models. Attribution models help determine which marketing efforts contributed to a sale or conversion. In AI marketing, a multi-touch attribution model might be more appropriate as it considers the multiple interactions a customer has with various touchpoints before converting. This model provides a more comprehensive view of the customer journey, highlighting the role of AI-driven touchpoints.

Machine learning algorithms themselves can assist in measuring ROI. Predictive analytics can forecast the potential revenue impact of AI strategies based on historical data. By simulating different scenarios, marketers can estimate the ROI of various AI applications, enabling more informed decision-making.

However, not all benefits are immediately measurable. Long-term impacts such as brand loyalty and reputation are crucial but take time to manifest. To account for these, marketers should consider adopting a longer-term view when calculating ROI. Periodic reviews and adjustments ensure that AI strategies are aligned with evolving business objectives.

Engaging stakeholders across departments can also enhance the accuracy of ROI measurements. Cross-functional collaboration ensures that all relevant data points are considered, providing a more complete picture of AI's impact. For instance, collaboration between the marketing and finance teams can help capture indirect savings, such as reduced customer service costs due to improved AI-driven customer support.

It's also essential to continuously optimize AI models to keep them effective. Post-implementation evaluation should be an ongoing process. Regularly updating algorithms and retraining models with fresh data can sustain or even improve ROI over time. Keeping up with technological advancements and industry trends ensures that your AI tools remain cutting-edge and competitive.

Moreover, transparency in metrics and methodology fosters trust and buy-in from stakeholders. Detailed reporting and clear communication about how ROI is measured can demystify AI for non-technical team members, encouraging broader acceptance and support for AI initiatives.

Let's not forget the ethical considerations in measuring ROI in AI marketing. Ethical AI ensures that all data points are collected and analyzed fairly, without bias or discrimination. Marketers should adhere to privacy regulations and ethical guidelines to maintain customer trust and avoid potential legal repercussions.

In ensuring ethical AI, consider how data is sourced and used. Transparency in data usage builds trust and can actually enhance the effectiveness of your AI models. For example, letting customers know how their data will improve their experience can result in increased willingness to share information, thereby improving the models' accuracy and effectiveness.

Case studies serve as valuable benchmarks for measuring ROI. By examining successful AI implementations in similar industries, marketers can gain insights into potential outcomes and identify best practices. These case studies often provide detailed ROI analyses, delineating both the financial gains and operational improvements attributable to AI.

ROI in AI marketing is not a one-time metric but a continuous loop that involves setting objectives, implementing solutions, measuring outcomes, and refining strategies. The iterative nature of AI—its ability to learn and improve over time—should be mirrored in your approach to measuring ROI. Continuous investment in data quality, model accuracy, and stakeholder engagement is essential for sustained success.

To wrap up, measuring ROI in AI marketing requires a multifaceted approach that balances quantitative metrics with qualitative insights. A clear alignment between AI initiatives and business objectives, combined with robust measurement techniques like A/B testing and attribution models, lays a strong foundation for accurate ROI calculations. Long-term impacts, ethical considerations, and continuous optimization further enhance the validity and relevance of your ROI measurements. By embracing these strategies, marketing professionals can not only justify their AI investments but also drive sustained success and innovation in an increasingly data-driven world.

CHAPTER 21:
COMMON CHALLENGES AND SOLUTIONS

Integrating artificial intelligence (AI) into marketing strategies offers transformative potential, but it's not without its complexities. Professionals often face a range of challenges that can impede their progress if not addressed effectively. In this chapter, we'll explore some of the most common obstacles encountered in AI-driven marketing and provide actionable solutions to overcome them.

One of the biggest hurdles is data quality and availability. AI algorithms thrive on data, but not all data is good data. Inconsistent, incomplete, or outdated data can skew insights and lead to ineffective strategies. To mitigate this, implementing a robust data governance framework is essential. Regular audits, validation processes, and data cleaning protocols ensure that the data feeding into your AI systems is accurate and reliable. Additionally, consider investing in data enrichment services that can fill in the gaps and enhance your existing datasets.

Another common challenge is the integration of AI tools with existing marketing technology stacks. Marketing professionals often work with a variety of platforms and tools, from CRM systems to email marketing software. Integrating new AI tools with these legacy systems can be daunting. To ease this process, start with a pilot program. Select a small, manageable portion of your marketing activities to test the new AI tool and gradually scale up. Moreover, ensure that your chosen AI solutions offer API integrations and robust customer support to facilitate seamless integration.

Understanding and interpreting AI-driven insights can also be intimidating. While AI can process vast amounts of data and generate insights, the outputs are often complex and require a certain level of expertise to interpret accurately. Training your team is crucial. Consider investing in AI education and training programs to upskill your marketing team. Workshops, online courses, and certifications can empower your team to understand AI insights and apply them effectively in your marketing strategies.

Cost is another significant barrier. Implementing AI solutions can be expensive, particularly for small businesses or startups with limited budgets. However, there's a growing number of affordable AI tools and platforms available. Cloud-based AI services offer scalable solutions that allow businesses to start small and expand as their budget allows. It's essential to perform a cost-benefit analysis before investing in AI tools. Determine the potential ROI by assessing how these tools will improve efficiency, customer engagement, and ultimately drive sales.

Privacy and ethical considerations also pose substantial challenges. AI systems often handle sensitive customer data, raising concerns about data privacy and security. To address these, comply with regulations such as GDPR and CCPA. Implement strong data protection measures, such as encryption and anonymization of customer data. Establish clear data handling policies and transparent communication with your customers about how their data is used. Ethics should be at the forefront of your AI strategy; develop ethical guidelines that govern the use of AI in your marketing activities.

Another challenge is maintaining the human touch in a technologically driven strategy. While AI can automate and optimize many marketing tasks, the human element is still crucial for creating authentic and relatable customer interactions. To keep this balance, use AI to augment rather than replace human efforts. For example, AI can handle routine customer service inquiries, freeing up human agents to tackle more complex issues and build deeper relationships with customers. Personalization should feel personal; use AI to provide insights and recommendations, but let human creativity and empathy shape the final output.

Bias in AI algorithms is a critical challenge that can undermine the effectiveness of your marketing strategies. AI systems are only as unbiased as the data they are trained on. If the training data contains biases, the AI system will perpetuate these biases in its outputs. Regularly audit your AI systems and datasets for biases. Implement fairness-aware machine learning techniques and involve diverse teams in the AI development process to mitigate these issues. It's also beneficial to have a feedback loop where users can report biased or unfair AI behavior, allowing for continual improvement and recalibration.

Deployment and scalability can be tricky, especially if you're dealing with rapid growth or seasonal fluctuations. AI systems need to be designed with scalability in mind. Cloud computing platforms provide scalable infrastructure that can handle varying workloads. Ensure that your AI solutions can scale up or down based on demand without compromising performance. Performance monitoring tools can help you track the system's efficiency and make necessary adjustments in real-time.

Lastly, measuring the success of AI implementations is crucial but often challenging. Many marketing teams struggle with defining the right metrics and KPIs to track AI's impact. Start by aligning your AI initiatives with your overall business goals. Determine clear, measurable objectives for your AI projects - whether it's increased customer engagement, higher conversion rates, or cost savings. Use these objectives to develop specific KPIs. Regularly review and optimize based on these metrics to ensure your AI efforts are delivering the desired outcomes.

In conclusion, while implementing AI in marketing comes with its set of challenges, understanding and addressing these obstacles can pave the way for successful AI integration. By focusing on data quality, seamless integration, proper training, cost management, privacy and ethics, maintaining the human touch, avoiding bias, ensuring scalability, and measuring success accurately, marketing professionals can harness the full potential of AI to drive innovation and growth. Keep these solutions in mind as you continue to explore the exciting world of AI-driven marketing.

CHAPTER 22:
FUTURE TRENDS IN AI MARKETING

The landscape of marketing is continually evolving, and AI is poised to be at the forefront of this transformation. The rapid advancements in artificial intelligence technologies offer unparalleled opportunities for marketers to innovate and refine their strategies. Let's delve into some of the most promising AI trends that are set to reshape the marketing arena.

First and foremost, the rise of hyper-personalization stands out as a key trend. With AI's ability to analyze vast amounts of data, marketers can now create highly personalized experiences tailored to individual customer preferences and behaviors. Unlike traditional segmentation methods, which often rely on broad demographic data, hyper-personalization leverages real-time data and sophisticated algorithms to deliver unique recommendations, products, and content. This shift ensures that each customer feels valued and understood, fostering deeper brand loyalty.

Moreover, AI-powered chatbots are becoming more advanced and intuitive. Far from the basic question-and-answer bots of the past, modern AI chatbots utilize natural language processing (NLP) and machine learning to understand and respond to complex customer queries. They can seamlessly handle a wide range of interactions, from simple inquiries to nuanced support issues, providing instant, 24/7 assistance. As chatbot technology continues to improve, these virtual assistants will play an even more integral role in customer service and engagement.

Another burgeoning trend is the integration of AI with voice search technology. Voice-activated assistants like Amazon's Alexa, Apple's Siri, and Google's Assistant are increasingly popular, changing the way consumers search for information and make purchases. This shift necessitates that marketers optimize their content for voice search, which often involves more conversational and question-based queries. AI tools can help in crafting this content, ensuring it aligns with the natural speech patterns of consumers.

In addition to voice search, visual search is gaining traction. Powered by AI, visual search allows users to upload an image to find similar products or information online. This technology is particularly powerful in industries like fashion and home décor, where visuals play a critical role in purchasing decisions. Companies can enhance their visual search capabilities through AI-driven image recognition and deep learning, making it easier for customers to find exactly what they're looking for.

Predictive analytics is another area where AI is making significant strides. By analyzing historical data and identifying patterns, predictive analytics can forecast future customer behaviors and trends. This ability allows marketers to anticipate customer needs, optimize inventory, and forecast sales with greater accuracy. As AI algorithms become more sophisticated, the predictive power of these tools will only increase, delivering even deeper insights into consumer behavior.

AI is also revolutionizing content creation. Algorithms can now generate high-quality, human-like content across various formats, including articles, videos, and social media posts. These AI-generated pieces are not just well-written but also optimized for search engines and tailored to specific audience segments. This capability allows marketers to scale their content efforts efficiently, ensuring a steady stream of engaging and relevant material.

Programmatic advertising, driven by AI, is automating the ad buying process. By leveraging AI tools to bid on ad spaces in real-time, marketers can effectively target their desired audience segments, improve ad performance, and optimize budgets. As AI's capabilities expand, programmatic advertising will become even more precise and efficient, reducing waste and maximizing return on investment.

Ethical AI marketing is another critical trend to watch. As AI tools become more pervasive, the ethical implications of data collection, analysis, and usage are under increasing scrutiny. Companies are faced with the challenge of balancing innovation with privacy and ethical considerations. Transparent data practices, robust security measures, and adherence to regulatory standards will be essential in maintaining consumer trust and leveraging AI responsibly.

Furthermore, augmented reality (AR) and virtual reality (VR) are set to revolutionize the way consumers interact with brands. AI-powered AR and VR experiences can create immersive, interactive environments that bring products to life in ways traditional media cannot. Whether it's trying on virtual clothing or exploring a virtual store, these technologies offer exciting new avenues for engagement and conversion.

Integration of AI with blockchain technology represents another exciting frontier. Blockchain's decentralized and secure nature complements AI's data-processing capabilities, ensuring data integrity and transparency. This synergy can enhance data-sharing protocols and offer more secure and verifiable marketing processes, fostering trust and collaboration between brands and consumers.

AI in influencer marketing is also evolving. AI tools can now identify and analyze influencers who align with a brand's values and audience. By examining engagement metrics, audience demographics, and content relevance, AI ensures that partnerships are more authentic and effective. This approach not only maximizes the impact of influencer campaigns but also helps in identifying niche influencers who might have previously gone unnoticed.

Finally, the shift towards omni-channel marketing has been accelerated by AI. Consumers today interact with brands through multiple touchpoints, and it's vital for these interactions to be seamless and consistent. AI can integrate data across various channels, ensuring a cohesive customer experience. From predicting the next best action in a customer's journey to personalizing interactions across devices, AI is the backbone of effective omni-channel strategies.

As we look to the future, it's clear that AI will continue to drive innovation in marketing. The ongoing development of AI technologies promises to unlock even more possibilities, empowering marketers to connect with their audiences in deeper and more meaningful ways. Staying ahead of these trends and embracing AI's potential will be crucial for marketers aiming to thrive in an increasingly competitive landscape.

CHAPTER 23:
INTEGRATING AI WITH TRADITIONAL MARKETING STRATEGIES

As we delve deeper into the digital age, melding the cutting-edge capabilities of artificial intelligence (AI) with traditional marketing strategies has become indispensable. It's not about choosing between AI and conventional methods, but rather fusing the two to create a harmonious and powerful marketing engine. This chapter focuses on how marketing professionals can seamlessly integrate AI with traditional strategies to elevate their campaigns and drive remarkable results.

Firstly, consider the role of AI in enhancing customer insights. Historically, marketers relied on surveys, focus groups, and demographic data to understand their target audience. These traditional approaches provided valuable insights but were often time-consuming and limited in scope. Enter AI, with its capability to analyze vast amounts of data in real-time. By leveraging AI algorithms, marketers can now identify patterns and trends that might have been impossible to discern through manual analysis.

For example, AI can analyze social media interactions, browsing behavior, and purchase history to provide a comprehensive and up-to-the-minute profile of customer preferences and interests. These insights allow marketers to fine-tune their campaigns, ensuring that their messages resonate more deeply with their audience. Integrating these AI-driven insights with traditional demographic analysis provides a richer, more nuanced understanding of customer behavior.

Moreover, AI significantly enhances the personalization of marketing efforts. While traditional marketing strategies could segment audiences into broad categories, AI allows for hyper-personalization. This means tailoring messages not just to target groups but to individual preferences. AI-powered recommendation engines, for instance, have revolutionized how brands suggest products. By analyzing user data, these engines predict what a customer is likely to buy next and present tailored suggestions, boosting conversion rates dramatically.

Imagine a traditional email marketing campaign. Without AI, marketers might segment their email lists based on general demographics like age or location. With AI, they can go a step further—analyzing past buying behavior, browsing patterns, and even the time of day the customer is most likely to engage. As a result, each email can be personalized to the individual recipient's preferences, leading to higher open and click-through rates.

AI doesn't just stop at personalization; it excels in optimizing marketing campaigns. Traditional A/B testing, an essential part of any marketer's toolkit, can be laborious and time-consuming. AI enhances this process with multi-armed bandit algorithms, which allow marketers to test multiple variables simultaneously and adjust in real-time. This means campaigns can be optimized on-the-fly, ensuring the best possible performance without the long wait times traditionally associated with A/B testing.

Furthermore, AI's role in automating repetitive tasks cannot be overstated. Traditional marketing strategies often involve labor-intensive processes like scheduling social media posts, managing email lists, and sorting through customer feedback. AI-powered tools can automate these tasks, freeing up valuable time for marketers to focus on more strategic activities.

Take social media management as an example. Traditional methods would require a dedicated team to schedule posts, respond to comments, and track engagement manually. With AI, these processes can be automated. AI tools can schedule posts at optimal times, respond to common customer inquiries through chatbots, and even provide sentiment analysis on customer feedback. This not only increases efficiency but also ensures consistency in brand messaging.

Another crucial area where AI integrates with traditional marketing is in decision-making. Marketing has always been a blend of art and science, relying on creativity as much as data analysis. AI can enhance the scientific aspect by providing data-driven insights, but it can also support the artistic side by generating creative content ideas. AI tools that analyze trending topics, popular keywords, and competitive content can provide marketers with a wellspring of inspiration for their campaigns.

For instance, a traditional content marketing strategy might involve brainstorming sessions and manual research. AI can supplement this by suggesting topics that are currently trending in the industry or by analyzing competitor content to find gaps and opportunities. This data-driven creativity ensures that marketing efforts are always relevant and engaging.

Integrating AI with traditional marketing also brings about a new level of measurability. Traditional marketing efforts often struggled with proving ROI, especially for brand awareness campaigns. AI analytics tools can track every interaction, from clicks and views to sales conversions, providing a comprehensive picture of a campaign's effectiveness. This level of transparency allows marketers to fine-tune their strategies continually and justify their marketing spend with data-backed results.

Let's not forget the enhanced customer experience. Traditional customer service models, while effective for their time, often involved long wait times and generic responses. AI, through chatbots and virtual assistants, can provide instant, personalized responses around the clock. Integrating these AI tools into your customer service strategy ensures that customers receive timely and accurate assistance, improving their overall experience with your brand.

For instance, consider a traditional retail store where customers might have to wait for a sales representative to become available. An AI-powered chatbot on the store's website can immediately answer queries about product availability, return policies, and more, providing instant satisfaction to the customer. This integration of AI not only enhances customer service but also frees up human representatives to handle more complex issues, thus improving the efficiency of the support team.

In summary, integrating AI with traditional marketing strategies is not just an option—it's a necessity in today's fast-paced, data-driven world. AI's ability to provide deep insights, personalize at scale, optimize campaigns in real-time, automate repetitive tasks, enhance creativity, measure results, and improve customer experience makes it an invaluable tool for any marketer. Embracing this integration ensures that your marketing efforts are not only keeping up with the times but are also pioneering new ways to engage and delight your audience.

Let's harness the power of AI while respecting the foundations built by traditional marketing strategies. This balanced approach will undoubtedly drive your marketing efforts to new heights, ensuring sustained success and growth in an ever-evolving landscape.

CHAPTER 24:
BUILDING A SKILLED AI MARKETING TEAM

One of the critical factors for leveraging the full potential of artificial intelligence (AI) in marketing lies in building a skilled AI marketing team. As AI continues to evolve, businesses must ensure their teams are adept at utilizing these advancements to stay ahead of the competition. The fusion of traditional marketing acumen and advanced AI skills creates a formidable force, capable of delivering unprecedented results. But, constructing such a team requires a thoughtful strategy.

Assessing Your Current Team

Before attracting new talent, it's crucial to assess your existing team's capabilities. Identify the skills within your team and determine the gaps that need to be filled. Some marketers might already have a foundational understanding of AI technologies, while others could excel in data analysis or digital strategy. By performing a comprehensive skills assessment, you can pinpoint the areas needing reinforcement and design a development plan that aligns with your organization's marketing goals.

The Essential Roles

When assembling an AI marketing team, specific roles are indispensable. Finding the right balance hinges on the scope of your marketing objectives and the complexity of your AI initiatives. Here are some key positions:

Data Scientists: These professionals play a crucial role in interpreting complex datasets and deriving actionable insights. Their expertise in machine learning algorithms and statistical models makes them the backbone of any AI marketing team.

Machine Learning Engineers: Focused on the development and deployment of AI models, machine learning engineers bridge the gap between theoretical AI applications and practical marketing strategies.

AI Strategists: This role involves crafting and executing AI-driven marketing strategies, ensuring they align with broader business objectives. They must have a keen understanding of both marketing principles and AI capabilities.

Content Creators: While creativity is paramount, content creators versed in AI tools can elevate marketing efforts. For instance, they can use AI for content optimization, ensuring it resonates with target audiences.

Data Analysts: These individuals scrutinize marketing campaigns, using data analytics to gauge their success. Proficiency with AI tools enables them to refine strategies based on quantifiable insights.

The Role of Continuous Learning

AI technology is in perpetual evolution, rendering continuous learning an imperative part of building a skilled team. Encourage your team to pursue certifications and courses in AI and machine learning. Platforms like Coursera, edX, and Udacity offer specialized programs tailored to different aspects of AI in marketing.

Moreover, regular workshops and seminars can keep the team updated on the latest trends and tools. By fostering a culture of continuous learning, you enable your team to adapt and thrive in a rapidly evolving landscape.

Cultivating a Collaborative Environment

The complexity of AI projects often requires cross-functional collaboration. Marketing professionals, data scientists, and machine learning engineers must work synergistically to achieve shared objectives. Establishing clear communication channels and fostering a collaborative environment ensures seamless integration of AI capabilities into marketing strategies.

Regular team meetings, collaborative project management tools, and an open-door policy can significantly enhance cooperation. Encourage team members to share their insights, challenges, and successes, fostering a culture of collective growth and innovation.

Balancing Creativity and Technology

While technical skills are essential, the importance of creativity should not be underestimated. AI can analyze data and predict trends, but it's creativity that breathes life into marketing campaigns. Striking a balance between technical proficiency and creative prowess ensures your team can craft compelling, data-driven marketing strategies.

For instance, a campaign might leverage AI to identify customer preferences while relying on creative talent to craft personalized content that resonates emotionally with the audience. This balance transforms data into engaging narratives, fostering stronger customer connections.

Leadership and Vision

Strong leadership is pivotal in guiding an AI marketing team towards success. Leaders must have a clear vision of how AI can enhance marketing efforts and the foresight to anticipate potential challenges. Effective leaders inspire their teams, providing direction and support while encouraging innovation.

Moreover, leaders should facilitate professional development opportunities and advocate for a forward-thinking mindset. By doing so, they ensure their teams remain agile and responsive to industry changes, driving sustained growth and success.

Measuring Success

Implementing AI-driven strategies requires robust measurement frameworks to evaluate success accurately. Establish clear key performance indicators (KPIs) to track the effectiveness of AI initiatives. These KPIs might include customer engagement rates, conversion rates, and ROI from AI-driven campaigns.

Regular performance reviews help identify areas for improvement and refine strategies accordingly. By continually monitoring and analyzing performance metrics, your team can fine-tune their approach and optimize outcomes.

Embracing Ethical AI Practices

Amidst the excitement of leveraging AI, ethical considerations must not be overlooked. Ensure your team adheres to ethical AI practices, including data privacy and avoiding biases in AI models. Transparency and accountability in AI applications build consumer trust and mitigate potential risks.

Formulating guidelines and providing ethical training equips your team to make responsible decisions. By prioritizing ethical AI practices, you safeguard your brand's integrity while driving successful marketing campaigns.

Attracting Top Talent

Securing top talent in a competitive landscape requires a strategic approach. Emphasize your commitment to innovation, continuous learning, and ethical AI practices in your recruitment efforts. Highlighting these aspects can attract professionals passionate about advancing their careers in a dynamic and forward-thinking environment.

Additionally, offering competitive compensation packages and opportunities for professional growth can make your organization more appealing to skilled candidates.

Nurturing Team Dynamics

Building a skilled AI marketing team goes beyond hiring the right individuals; nurturing team dynamics is equally vital. Invest in team-building activities and social events to foster camaraderie and trust. A cohesive team with strong interpersonal relationships is more likely to collaborate effectively and achieve common goals.

Promote diversity and inclusivity within your team, as varied perspectives can lead to more innovative solutions. By valuing each team member's unique contributions, you cultivate a positive and productive work environment.

In conclusion, building a skilled AI marketing team is a multi-faceted endeavor requiring a blend of strategic planning, continuous learning, and strong leadership. By focusing on these key elements, you can assemble a team poised to harness the power of AI, driving transformative marketing results and setting your organization on a path to sustained success. As AI continues to shape the future of marketing, your team's ability to adapt and innovate will be the cornerstone of your competitive advantage.

CHAPTER 25:
DEVELOPING AN AI-DRIVEN
MARKETING STRATEGY

When it comes to crafting an AI-driven marketing strategy, the starting point is to recognize that AI isn't just a trendy buzzword. It's a transformative tool that can elevate your marketing efforts to new heights. The integration of AI into your marketing strategy is about precision, personalization, and creating engaging customer experiences that drive tangible results.

First things first, you need a clearly defined objective. What do you aim to achieve with your AI-driven marketing strategy? Is it to enhance customer engagement, increase sales, or optimize marketing operations? Establishing your goals from the outset will guide the AI technologies you choose and the data you need to collect. Setting a clear objective is crucial, as it aligns your team and resources towards a common purpose.

Once you've set your objectives, it's time to harness the power of data. Data is the lifeblood of AI, and without it, your AI initiatives will fall flat. The next step is collecting high-quality data from various sources: social media platforms, customer transactions, website behavior, CRM systems, and so forth. The more accurate and comprehensive your data, the better your AI models will perform. Consider using tools like big data platforms to gather and process this information.

With data in hand, the focus shifts to selecting the right AI technologies. From machine learning algorithms that predict customer behavior to natural language processing tools that enhance content creation, the choice of AI tools should align with your marketing goals. Technologies like recommendation systems, chatbots, and predictive analytics can all play pivotal roles in your strategy, each offering unique advantages.

Implementation is where the rubber meets the road. Begin by integrating AI tools into your existing marketing infrastructure. For example, you could embed AI-powered recommendation engines into your e-commerce site to offer personalized product suggestions. Or, deploy chatbots on your website for real-time customer support. The key here is to ensure seamless integration, so that AI augments rather than disrupts your current workflows.

It's important to remember that AI is not a set-it-and-forget-it solution. Regular monitoring and optimization are essential to its success. Utilize analytics dashboards to track the performance of your AI tools and gather insights. Are your AI-driven email campaigns yielding higher open rates? Is your chatbot resolving customer issues efficiently? These metrics will help you fine-tune your strategy and improve outcomes over time.

Don't underestimate the power of experimenting. AI provides an excellent platform for A/B testing and other experimental methods. You can test different variables such as content, timing, and audience segments to see what resonates best with your customers. This iterative approach allows for continuous improvement, ensuring that your marketing efforts evolve in line with customer preferences and behaviors.

Another critical element is collaboration. Developing an AI-driven marketing strategy isn't solely the responsibility of the marketing department. It requires cross-functional collaboration involving data scientists, engineers, creatives, and business strategists. By pooling expertise from various domains, you create a cohesive strategy that leverages AI to its fullest potential.

Ethics and transparency should also be integral components of your AI strategy. With growing concerns about data privacy and algorithmic bias, it's crucial to adopt ethical considerations. Be transparent with your customers about how their data is being used and ensure compliance with data protection regulations like GDPR. Ethical AI practices build trust and foster customer loyalty, which are invaluable assets in a competitive market landscape.

Equally important is scalability. As your marketing needs grow, your AI capabilities should evolve proportionately. Scalability involves both technological and human resources. Ensure that your AI infrastructure can handle increasing data volumes and complex algorithms. Simultaneously, invest in upskilling your team to keep pace with the latest AI advancements. A scalable strategy positions you to adapt quickly to market changes and emerging opportunities.

Ultimately, a successful AI-driven marketing strategy is one that balances innovation with operational efficiency. It leverages AI to make smarter decisions, enhances customer experiences, and drives business growth. While the technology may be complex, the guiding principles are straightforward: clear objectives, quality data, the right tools, seamless integration, continuous optimization, collaboration, ethics, and scalability.

In conclusion, developing an AI-driven marketing strategy entails a blend of strategic planning, technological know-how, and adaptive execution. By following these steps, you're not just keeping up with the times; you're positioning your organization to lead in a data-driven marketing future. AI is not just a tool—it's your competitive edge.

Conclusion

As we draw to a close, it's evident that the intersection of artificial intelligence and marketing heralds a transformative era for the industry. By blending the analytical precision of AI with the creativity and intuition inherent to marketing professionals, the potential for innovation and success is boundless. This book has served as a guide through the evolving landscape of AI marketing, offering insights and practical techniques designed to empower you to integrate AI effectively into your strategies.

Throughout the chapters, we delved into a myriad of ways AI can revolutionize marketing practices. From understanding the basics of AI to exploring its advances in data-driven insights, customer segmentation, and targeted personalization, each section illuminated a different aspect of this multifaceted technology. The robust discussions around automated marketing campaigns, chatbots, and predictive analytics underscored the dynamic capabilities of AI in optimizing and streamlining marketing efforts. These explorations have laid the groundwork for you to harness AI's potential in creating more impactful marketing strategies.

One of the fundamental takeaways is the importance of data. In the AI realm, data is the lifeblood that fuels the sophisticated algorithms and models that drive decision-making. Effective data collection and analysis open the door to deeper consumer insights and more accurate market predictions. As marketing professionals, embracing a data-centric approach can lead to more effective strategies that resonate with your target audience on a more profound level.

The advent of AI has also ushered in new levels of personalization and customer engagement. By leveraging AI, marketers can craft bespoke experiences that cater uniquely to each individual customer. Whether through advanced personalization techniques or the nuanced automation of customer interactions, AI offers tools to enhance the customer journey meaningfully. The benefits are clear: higher customer satisfaction, improved loyalty, and ultimately, better business outcomes.

However, none of these advancements come without their own set of challenges. The ethics and privacy considerations associated with AI in marketing cannot be overstated. As you integrate AI into your marketing strategies, it's crucial to maintain a balance between leveraging data for insight and respecting consumer privacy. Building transparent, ethical practices will not only protect your brand but will also foster trust and loyalty among your customers.

Moreover, the need for building a skilled AI marketing team is paramount. The successful implementation of AI in marketing isn't just about the technology itself but the people who wield it. Investing in training and development to cultivate a team proficient in both marketing know-how and AI technologies is critical. This synergy of skills will enable your organization to unlock AI's full potential and keep you ahead of the competition.

In predicting future trends, it's clear that AI's role in marketing will only grow. Future innovations will likely bring even more sophisticated tools and platforms, further pushing the boundaries of what's possible. As AI continues to evolve, staying informed and adaptable will be key to maintaining a competitive edge. This ongoing evolution calls for a mindset of continuous learning and readiness to adopt emerging technologies.

Your journey with AI in marketing doesn't end here. As this book has repeatedly emphasized, the effective application of AI is an ongoing process that requires agility, creativity, and a commitment to data-driven excellence. Whether you are enhancing customer loyalty programs, leveraging predictive analytics, or optimizing advertising strategies, the principles and insights outlined in these chapters serve as a solid foundation for your AI marketing endeavors.

To conclude, the fusion of AI and marketing isn't merely a trend but a paradigm shift. It promises more than just enhanced efficiencies and data-driven insights—it's about crafting richer, more personalized experiences for customers, driving engagement, and ultimately delivering measurable results. The possibilities are as vast as they are exciting, offering a new frontier for marketing innovation.

As you move forward, remember to maintain a strategic vision, always aligning technological capabilities with your underlying marketing goals. Stay curious, ethical, and data-informed, and your efforts to integrate AI into your marketing strategies will not only be fruitful but transformative. The future of marketing lies at the crossroads of human creativity and artificial intelligence, and your role in shaping that future is more critical than ever. Embrace the journey with confidence and foresight, and the rewards will undoubtedly follow.

APPENDIX A:
APPENDIX

This appendix serves as a supplementary section designed to enrich your understanding of AI in marketing. It provides additional resources and readings that enhance your grasp on the principles discussed throughout the book. From suggested readings to a glossary of key terms, this appendix is crafted to be a practical toolkit for any marketing professional aiming to integrate AI into their strategies effectively.

Suggested Readings

As you evolve your knowledge in AI marketing, continuous learning is crucial. Below is a curated list of books, articles, and papers that provide deeper insights into various facets of AI in marketing:

- **"Prediction Machines: The Simple Economics of Artificial Intelligence"** by Ajay Agrawal, Joshua Gans, and Avi Goldfarb

- **"Artificial Intelligence in Practice: How 50 Successful Companies Used AI and Machine Learning to Solve Problems"** by Bernard Marr

- **"Marketing Rebellion: The Most Human Company Wins"** by Mark Schaefer

- **"Human + Machine: Reimagining Work in the Age of AI"** by Paul R. Daugherty and H. James Wilson

- **Harvard Business Review Articles** on AI and Machine Learning in Marketing

These readings will not only complement the themes and strategies discussed in this book but will also keep you abreast with emerging trends and concepts in AI marketing.

Glossary of Terms

The glossary includes definitions of essential terms and concepts you encountered in the book. It is structured to be a quick reference guide:

- **Algorithm**: A set of rules or processes followed by a computer in performing problem-solving operations.

- **Artificial Intelligence (AI)**: The simulation of human intelligence processes by machines, especially computer systems.

- **Machine Learning (ML)**: A subset of AI that involves the development of algorithms that enable computers to learn from and make decisions based on data.

- **Neural Network**: A series of algorithms designed to recognize patterns, mimicking the neural pathways in the human brain.

- **Predictive Analytics**: Techniques that analyze current and historical facts to make predictions about future or otherwise unknown events.

- **Sentiment Analysis**: The use of natural language processing, text analysis, and computational linguistics to identify and extract subjective information from source materials.

- **Natural Language Processing (NLP)**: A field of AI that gives machines the ability to read, understand, and derive meaning from human languages.

This glossary is intended to provide concise and clear definitions, helping you to quickly revisit and grasp terms as you apply AI concepts to your marketing strategies.

Resources and Tools

In the fast-paced world of AI marketing, leveraging the right tools can make a significant difference. Here are some recommended platforms and resources:

- **Hootsuite**: Social media management tool that integrates AI to streamline content scheduling and performance analysis.

- **HubSpot**: A comprehensive inbound marketing, sales, and service software platform with AI-driven features.

- **Google Analytics**: A robust tool for analyzing web traffic and performance metrics, supported by machine learning capabilities.

- **IBM Watson**: A suite of AI tools from IBM that can be used to enhance marketing analytics, automation, and campaign optimization.

- **Marketo**: A marketing automation platform that offers tools for email marketing, lead management, and analytics.

By utilizing these resources and tools, you'll be better equipped to implement AI-driven marketing campaigns that deliver tangible results.

In conclusion, this appendix is designed to be a practical resource that complements the core content of the book. It provides supplementary information, key definitions, and valuable tools to support your journey in integrating AI into your marketing practices.

Suggested Readings

The journey of integrating artificial intelligence into marketing strategies is both exciting and challenging. It requires constant learning and adaptation. To aid in this endeavor, here is a curated list of suggested readings that will expand your understanding and keep you updated with the latest advancements. These resources cover a broad spectrum of topics relevant to AI in marketing, providing insights from industry experts, data scientists, and marketers who have successfully navigated the AI landscape.

We begin with books that delve into the fundamentals and the transformative power of AI. "Prediction Machines: The Simple Economics of Artificial Intelligence" by Ajay Agrawal, Joshua Gans, and Avi Goldfarb is a crucial read. It breaks down the economic implications of AI, making complex concepts accessible. For those who prefer a more comprehensive guide, "Artificial Intelligence: A Guide for Thinking Humans" by Melanie Mitchell provides an overview of AI's history, current state, and future potential, all while posing critical questions about the ethical and societal impacts of AI.

For a focus on data-driven insights and analytics, "Data Science for Business: What You Need to Know about Data Mining and Data-Analytic Thinking" by Foster Provost and Tom Fawcett is indispensable. This book equips you with the necessary tools and frameworks to leverage data effectively. "Competing on Analytics: The New Science of Winning" by Thomas H. Davenport and Jeanne G. Harris is another essential read, illustrating how leading organizations use analytics to outstrip their competitors.

To understand how AI influences customer segmentation and targeting, "Marketing 4.0: Moving from Traditional to Digital" by Philip Kotler, Hermawan Kartajaya, and Iwan Setiawan blends traditional marketing principles with digital advancements. This book offers practical insights and strategies for navigating the digital landscape.

Similarly, "Segmentation, Revenue Management and Pricing Analytics" by Tudor Bodea and Mark Ferguson gives an in-depth look at modern segmentation techniques essential for maximizing revenue.

Customer experience and personalization are at the heart of AI in marketing. "The Power of Customer Experience: How to Use Customer Journey Mapping to Drive Customer Advocacy" by Colin Shaw and Ryan Hamilton is key for understanding the pivotal role of customer experience. For advanced personalization strategies, "One-to-One Personalization in the Age of Machine Learning" by Karl Wirth and Katie Sweetman covers cutting-edge techniques and methodologies.

Automated marketing campaigns have revolutionized the way we interact with customers. "Marketing Automation For Dummies" by Mathew Sweezey is a comprehensive guide that demystifies automation. Another notable mention is "The Automated Marketing Handbook: How to Harness the Power of AI and Machine Learning" by Yulia Barnakova, which dives into the specifics of automating various aspects of your marketing strategy.

Chatbots and customer service are another crucial area. "Voicebot and Chatbot Design: Flexible Conversational Interfaces with Amazon Alexa, Google Home, and Facebook Messenger" by Rachel Batish is invaluable for designing effective chatbot experiences. "Conversational Marketing: How the World's Fastest Growing Companies Use Chatbots to Generate Leads 24/7/365" by David Cancel and Dave Gerhardt provides practical insights directly from industry leaders.

Predictive analytics can drive powerful results through foresight. "Predictive Analytics: The Power to Predict Who Will Click, Buy, Lie, or Die" by Eric Siegel offers a compelling introduction to the power of predictive analytics. It's a great resource to understand how predictions can be used effectively in marketing.

AI-driven content creation is transforming the landscape of content marketing. "The Content Code: Six Essential Strategies to Ignite Your Content, Your Marketing, and Your Business" by Mark Schaefer helps marketers understand how to create content that stands out in a crowded digital space. Furthermore, "Everybody Writes: Your Go-To Guide to Creating Ridiculously Good Content" by Ann Handley emphasizes the power of compelling content in the age of AI.

For search engine optimization (SEO) and AI, "The Art of SEO: Mastering Search Engine Optimization" by Eric Enge, Stephan Spencer, and Jesse Stricchiola provides comprehensive strategies that now integrate with AI. "SEO 2023: Learn Search Engine Optimization with Smart Internet Marketing Strategies" by Adam Clarke also gives a good overview of modern SEO practices, including how AI can enhance these strategies.

In the realm of AI in advertising, "Killing Marketing: How Innovative Businesses Are Turning Marketing Cost into Profit" by Joe Pulizzi and Robert Rose explores new advertising models and strategies. It focuses on transforming marketing from a cost center to a revenue-generating function. For inclusion of programmatic advertising insights, "Programmatic Advertising: The Successful Transformation to Automated, Data-Driven Marketing in Real-Time" by Oliver Busch offers guidelines on executing target-specific, automated ads.

Influencer marketing powered by AI is another rich field. "Influencer: Building Your Personal Brand in the Age of Social Media" by Brittany Hennessy explains the dynamics of influencer marketing and how AI can amplify these efforts. "The Age of Influence: The Power of Influencers to Elevate Your Brand" by Neal Schaffer gives additional strategies for leveraging influencers with the support of AI tools.

Building and enhancing customer loyalty programs can be significantly amplified by AI. "The Loyalty Leap: Turning Customer Information into Customer Intimacy" by Bryan Pearson discusses how to use customer data to create more effective loyalty programs. "Hooked: How to Build Habit-Forming Products" by Nir Eyal also offers insights into creating products and programs that keep customers engaged and loyal.

Sentiment analysis is a powerful tool in the marketer's arsenal. "Sentiment Analysis for Social Media" by Carlos A. Iglesias and Arianne Reith provides technical and practical insights into conducting sentiment analysis. "The Social Media Bible: Tactics, Tools, and Strategies for Business Success" by Lon Safko touches on broader social media strategies, including sentiment analysis as a pivotal component.

Market research driven by AI insights can unveil transformative opportunities. "The Market Research Toolbox: A Concise Guide for Beginners" by Edward F. McQuarrie introduces traditional and modern methods of market research. Complementing this, "Marketing Research: An Applied Orientation" by Naresh K. Malhotra extends the exploration to advanced research techniques enhanced by AI.

Ethics and privacy in the realm of AI marketing cannot be overlooked. "Weapons of Math Destruction: How Big Data Increases Inequality and Threatens Democracy" by Cathy O'Neil is crucial for understanding the ethical implications of data-driven decisions. "Privacy and Freedom" by Alan Westin lays foundational concepts of privacy, which are more pertinent than ever in the age of AI.

To navigate the plethora of tools and platforms available for AI marketing, "AI for Marketing and Product Innovation: Powerful New Tools for Predicting Trends, Connecting with Customers, and Closing Sales" by A. K. Pradeep, Andrew Appel, and Stan Sthanunathan is invaluable. This book provides a roadmap for leveraging current AI tools effectively.

For those implementing AI in small businesses, "AI for

GLOSSARY OF TERMS

U nderstanding the various terms and concepts within the realm of AI and marketing is crucial to effectively leveraging these technologies. Below is a comprehensive glossary designed to clarify key terminology used throughout this book:

Artificial Intelligence (AI): The simulation of human intelligence processes by machines, especially computer systems. Common AI applications include expert systems, natural language processing (NLP), and machine vision.

Algorithm: A set of rules or processes followed in problem-solving operations, often by a computer.

Big Data: Large and complex datasets that traditional data-processing software cannot manage. In marketing, big data helps identify patterns, trends, and associations, particularly relating to human behavior and interactions.

Chatbot: An AI program designed to simulate conversation with human users, especially over the internet, for purposes such as customer service or information acquisition.

Customer Segmentation: The practice of dividing a customer base into groups of individuals that are similar in specific ways, such as age, gender, interests, purchasing habits, etc.

Data-Driven Marketing: Marketing strategies and tactics that rely on data analytics to drive decisions and measure performance.

Machine Learning (ML): A subset of AI that involves the development of algorithms that allow computers to learn from and make predictions or decisions based on data.

Natural Language Processing (NLP): A branch of AI that helps computers understand, interpret, and respond to human language in a valuable way.

Personalization: The process of tailoring content, recommendations, or marketing messages to individual users based on their behavior, preferences, and data analytics.

Predictive Analytics: The use of statistical algorithms and machine learning techniques to identify the likelihood of future outcomes based on historical data.

Programmatic Advertising: Automated buying and selling of online advertising that uses AI to optimize ad placements and target audience based on data analytics.

ROI (Return on Investment): A performance measure used to evaluate the efficiency or profitability of an investment, calculated by dividing the net profit by the initial cost of the investment.

Sentiment Analysis: A technique used to determine the emotional tone behind a series of words, utilized in marketing to gauge customer opinions and feelings about products, services, or brands.

SEO (Search Engine Optimization): The practice of increasing the quantity and quality of traffic to a website through organic search engine results.

Social Media Automation: The use of tools and platforms to automate social media activities such as content scheduling, post creation, and audience engagement, helping to streamline efforts and improve efficiency.

Resources and Tools

Delving into AI marketing requires a firm grasp of the specialized resources and tools at your disposal. This section seeks to equip you with a robust toolkit to seamlessly integrate artificial intelligence into your marketing strategies, catalyzing success and customer engagement.

First and foremost, data management platforms (DMPs) provide the bedrock for most AI-driven marketing strategies. These platforms amalgamate customer data from a multitude of sources, offering a panoramic view that allows for refined segmentation and precise targeting. Think of them as the foundation on which your AI systems can build sophisticated models to understand customer behavior. Popular DMPs, such as Adobe Audience Manager and Oracle BlueKai, merge diverse datasets, thus enabling more accurate predictions and effective campaigns.

Machine Learning Libraries

Machine learning libraries and frameworks are indispensable for any marketing professional aiming to dive deep into AI. Libraries like TensorFlow, PyTorch, and scikit-learn are industry standards, providing you the tools to build and experiment with your own algorithms. These libraries offer pre-built models and extensive documentation, making it easier to implement AI in marketing initiatives.

Natural Language Processing Tools

Natural Language Processing (NLP) is another critical resource, especially for tasks like sentiment analysis and chatbot development. Tools like Google's BERT and OpenAI's GPT-3 can process vast collections of text data, extracting valuable insights regarding customer sentiments and preferences. These insights can then be translated into personalized marketing messages or efficient customer service responses.

Customer Relationship Management Systems

Incorporating AI into your Customer Relationship Management (CRM) system is a game-changer. CRM platforms like Salesforce Einstein and HubSpot offer AI capabilities that help predict customer needs, streamline sales processes, and foster stronger relationships. These integrations provide real-time analytics and recommendations, thus enhancing decision-making and marketing strategy refinement.

Automated Campaign Tools

Automated campaign management tools like Marketo and Mailchimp leverage AI to optimize your marketing efforts, from email marketing to social media engagement. They use machine learning algorithms to analyze past campaign performance, predict future trends, and adjust your strategy accordingly. This level of automation not only saves time but also increases efficiency and effectiveness.

Customer Data Platforms

Customer Data Platforms (CDPs) such as Segment and Tealium enable marketers to manage and analyze data across touchpoints. These platforms integrate seamlessly with other AI tools, offering enhanced data unification and accessibility. This integration helps in driving more targeted and personalized marketing efforts, as well as optimizing resource allocation.

AI Content Creation Tools

For content creation, AI-powered tools like Copy.ai and Jasper (formerly Jarvis.ai) are invaluable. These platforms generate relevant and engaging content based on your input, helping you maintain a consistent and compelling voice across various marketing channels. Leveraging these tools allows you to focus more on strategy and creativity, rather than the nitty-gritty of content generation.

Predictive Analytics Platforms

Predictive analytics is pivotal in foreseeing market trends and customer behaviors. Platforms like IBM Watson Analytics and RapidMiner utilize sophisticated algorithms to provide actionable insights based on historical data. These insights can guide your marketing efforts, from product development to customer retention strategies.

Sentiment Analysis Tools

Understanding customer sentiment is quintessential for creating resonant marketing messages. Tools like Lexalytics and MonkeyLearn enable you to conduct in-depth sentiment analysis on social media interactions, customer reviews, and other textual data. This helps you gauge public opinion and tailor your campaigns to better meet customer expectations.

AI-Powered Analytics Platforms

AI-powered analytics platforms such as Google Analytics 360 and Adobe Analytics leverage machine learning to provide deeper insights into customer behavior. They help in uncovering patterns and trends that might not be apparent through manual analysis. These insights are crucial for refining your marketing strategies and making data-driven decisions.

Visualization Tools

Effective data visualization tools like Tableau and Power BI are indispensable for interpreting complex datasets. These platforms translate raw data into easily understandable visual formats, allowing you to present your findings compellingly to stakeholders. Additionally, they offer interactive dashboards that can be customized to fit your specific needs.

Chatbot Development Platforms

Platforms like Dialogflow and Microsoft Bot Framework simplify the process of developing intelligent chatbots. These tools provide pre-built templates and integrations with various messaging apps, making it easier to deploy chatbots that enhance customer service and engagement. Moreover, they offer analytics to continually improve chatbot performance.

Marketing Automation Suites

Comprehensive marketing automation suites like HubSpot and Pardot integrate a range of tools for email marketing, social media scheduling, lead generation, and analytics. These suites often come with AI capabilities that optimize each aspect of your marketing efforts, from segmenting your audience to personalizing content and measuring ROI.

In summary, equipping yourself with the right resources and tools is essential for leveraging AI in marketing. By integrating these technologies, you can enhance efficiency, drive personalization, and ultimately achieve superior customer engagement and measurable marketing outcomes.